THE SCHOOL MATHEMATICS PROJECT

K̶.̶M̶.̶Wigle S

When the S.M.P. was founded in 1961, its objective was to devise radically new mathematics courses, with accompanying G.C.E. syllabuses and examinations, which would reflect, more adequately than did the traditional syllabuses, the up-to-date nature and usages of mathematics.

The first stage of this objective is now more or less complete. *Books 1–5* form the main series of pupils' texts, starting at the age of 11 + and leading to the O-level examination in 'S.M.P. Mathematics', while *Books 3T, 4* and *5* give a three-year course to the same O-level examination. (*Books T* and *T4*, together with their Supplement, represent the first attempt at this three-year course, but they may be regarded as obsolete.) *Advanced Mathematics Books 1–4* cover the syllabus for the A-level examination in 'S.M.P. Mathematics' and five shorter texts cover the material of various sections of the A-level examination in 'S.M.P. Further Mathematics'. There are two books for 'S.M.P. Additional Mathematics' at O-level. Every book is accompanied by a Teacher's Guide.

For the convenience of schools, the S.M.P. has an arrangement whereby its examinations are made available by every G.C.E. Examining Board, and it is most grateful to the Secretaries of the eight Boards for their cooperation in this. At the same time, most Boards now offer their own syllabuses in 'modern mathematics' for which the S.M.P. texts are suitable.

By 1967, it had become clear from experience in comprehensive schools that the mathematical content of the S.M.P. texts was suitable for a much wider range of pupil than had been originally anticipated, but that the presentation needed adaptation. Thus it was decided to produce a new series, *Books A–H*, which could serve as a secondary school course starting at the age of 11 +. These books are specially suitable for pupils aiming at a C.S.E. examination; however, the framework of the C.S.E. examinations is such that it is inappropriate for the S.M.P. to offer its own examination as it does for the G.C.E.

The completion of all these books does not mean that the S.M.P. has no more to offer to the cause of curriculum research. The team of S.M.P. writers, now numbering some thirty school and university mathematicians, is continually testing and revising old work and preparing for new. At the same time, the effectiveness of the S.M.P.'s work depends, as it always has done, on obtaining reactions from active teachers – and also from pupils – in the classroom. Readers of the texts can therefore send their comments to the S.M.P. in the knowledge that they will be warmly welcomed.

Finally, the year-by-year activity of the S.M.P. is recorded in the annual Director's Reports which readers are encouraged to obtain on request to the S.M.P. Office at Westfield College, University of London, Kidderpore Avenue, Hampstead, London NW3 7ST.

D1714020

ACKNOWLEDGEMENTS

The principal authors, on whose contributions the S.M.P. texts are largely based, are named in the annual Reports. Many other authors have also provided original material, and still more have been directly involved in the revision of draft versions of chapters and books. The Project gratefully acknowledges the contributions which they and their schools have made.

This book – *Book H* – has been written by

Joyce Harris   R. W. Strong
D. A. Hobbs   Thelma Wilson
K. Lewis

and edited by Elizabeth Smith.

The Project owes a great deal to its Secretary, Miss Jacqueline Sinfield, for her careful typing and assistance in connection with this book.

We would especially thank Professor J. V. Armitage for the advice he has given on the fundamental mathematics of the course.

We are grateful to the Southern Regional Examinations Board and to the Oxford and Cambridge Schools Examination Board for permission to use questions from their examination papers.

Some of the drawings at the chapter openings in this book are by Ken Vail.

We are much indebted to the Cambridge University Press for their cooperation and help at all times.

THE SCHOOL MATHEMATICS PROJECT

BOOK H

CAMBRIDGE
AT THE UNIVERSITY PRESS

1972

Preface

Book H is the final book of a series which has been designed to cover a course suitable for those pupils wishing to take a C.S.E. examination on one of the reformed mathematics syllabuses. However, the books have proved suitable for a wider range of pupil than anticipated and there are now three extension books in preparation for potential O-level candidates. These books will lead on from *Book G* (thereby forming a ten-book course) and will cover the syllabus of the O-level examination in SMP Mathematics. Also in preparation is a series of work-cards based on *Books A* and *B*, which can be used as an alternative to the books and which are particularly suitable for use in mixed ability classes.

As this book is the last of a series for pupils aiming at a C.S.E. examination, it contains nine review chapters as well as seven chapters (including the Prelude) of new work. The Prelude gives pupils experience with simple three-dimensional work.

The chapter on gradients requires pupils to find the gradients of straight line graphs and to interpret their meaning in a variety of situations. Chapter 4, which deals with areas under linear and non-linear graphs, involves more graphical interpretation. The chapter on linear programming is restricted to problems with not more than three conditions and does not involve maximizing or minimizing.

Chapter 2, Combined Transformations, continues the work on matrices and transformations done in *Book G*. The statistics chapter also follows up work from *Book G* and considers the median and inter-quartile range from a cumulative frequency curve. The trigonometry chapter picks up the work on gradients in this book as a lead-in to tangents.

In writing the review chapters, the authors have aimed at as much pupil participation as possible, for it is by working and thinking for themselves, and not just reading, that pupils learn and retain the most. Exercise material on each of the review chapters is collected together at the back of the book, and is followed by some general miscellaneous exercises.

Answers to exercises are not printed at the end of this book, but are contained in the companion *Teacher's Guide* which gives a detailed commentary on the pupil's text. In this series, the answers and commentary are interleaved with the text.

Contents

Contents

Prelude

THREE DIMENSIONS

Each of the drawings in Figure 1 shows a thin pole stuck into the ground.

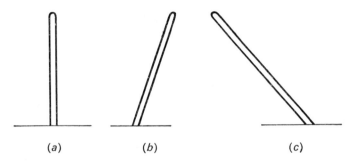

(a)　　　　　　(b)　　　　　　(c)

Fig. 1

Basil Brayne said:

Figure 1 (a) shows an upright pole,

Figure 1 (b) shows a pole making an angle of about 72° with the ground,

Figure 1 (c) shows a pole making an angle of about 50° with the ground.

Was he right?

Think about it before you turn over.

1

Prelude

In fact Basil Brayne was wrong. The drawings show the same pole. The angle depends on where you look from.

Try it using a pen with one end on your paper.

This Prelude is about *three-dimensional geometry*. As you may have just seen, it is not easy to visualize objects in three dimensions. You will find that it will help if you have a model available. A box, such as a shoe box, would be useful in the first investigations. (It will need a top on it.)

Investigation 1

Figure 2 shows a room. Fred the mathematical fly is in a top corner at *F*. Spike the spider is in a bottom corner at *S*.

Spike decides to stalk Fred by making his way along the edges of the room.

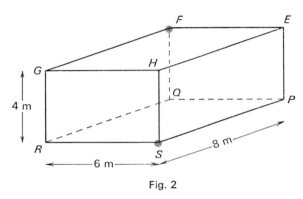

Fig. 2

(*a*) What is the shortest distance along the edges? How many such shortest routes are available?

(*b*) There are other longer routes. Find the length of the next longest route. How many routes are there of this length?

(*c*) Investigate the lengths of all the other possible routes, and find how many there are of each. (*Note:* Spike never goes through the same corner twice in any one attack on Fred.)

Investigation 2

Spike versus Fred again, but with different rules.

This time Spike walks diagonally across the carpet and then up the wall. See Figure 3 (*a*).

To find how far he goes, look at Figure 3 (*b*) which shows a fly's eye view of the floor. Use Pythagoras's rule to find the diagonal distance.

(*a*) How far does Spike go during this attack?

(*b*) There are two other routes of different lengths involving a diagonal and one edge. Find their lengths.

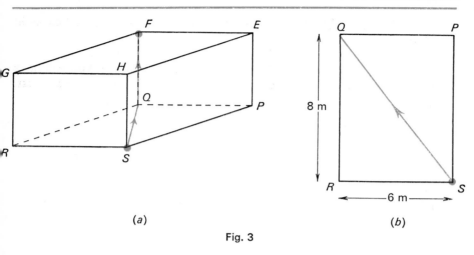

(a)   (b)

Fig. 3

Investigation 3

Fred sometimes gets his revenge. When Spike is asleep Fred buzzes him. How far does Fred have to fly in order to reach Spike? It will help if you cut a triangle of paper as shown in Figure 4.

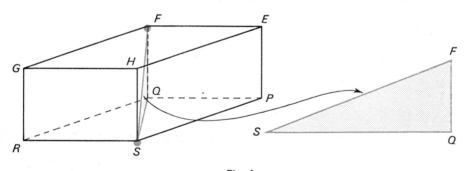

Fig. 4

The length of the base of this triangle is just the length of a diagonal of the floor – and you calculated this in Investigation 2. The height of the triangle is 4 m, the height of the room. Use Pythagoras's rule to find the distance which Fred has to fly.

Investigation 4

Spike decides to take the shortest route to Fred's corner, over the walls and over the floor or the ceiling, as necessary.
    The problem is to find the length of this shortest route.
    Try to work it out before you turn over.

It will help to find the shortest route if you open out your box as in Figure 5.

The three points marked *F* fold up to make Fred's corner.

The shortest distance for Spike will be in a straight line. You will have to decide which of the three distances shown in Figure 5 is the shortest. You should be able to do it by using Pythagoras's rule.

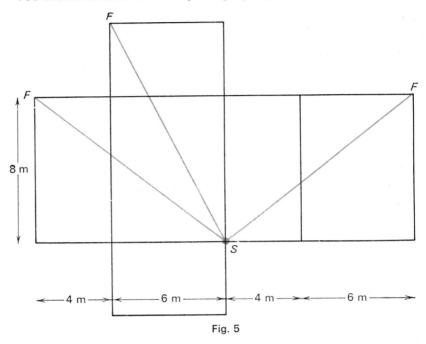

Fig. 5

Investigation 5: Fred and a wedge

Fred is at one corner of a wedge, and Spike at another. See Figure 6.

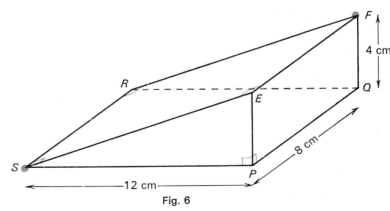

Fig. 6

(*a*) Calculate all the possible distances from *S* to *F* along the edges.

(*b*) Calculate the direct distance across the sloping face.

4

Investigation 6: How Fred's love of baked beans leads to his untimely death

Fred is at the top edge of a tin of baked beans. Spike is vertically below him at the bottom edge (see Figure 7).

Spike craftily takes a diagonal route and catches Fred by surprise. There is a struggle. Spike wins. Fred is dead.

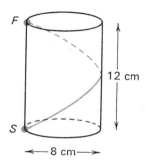

12 cm

8 cm

Fig. 7

Calculate how far Spike walked. If you have difficulty read on.

To find how far Spike goes imagine that the label on the tin is opened out. See Figure 8.

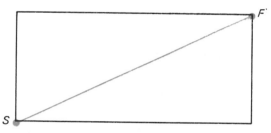

Fig. 8

Calculate first the length of the label. (Take π as 3.)
Then use Pythagoras's rule to find the length of Spike's route.

Some further 'box' problems

1   If, in Investigation 4, Spike had been at the middle of the 6 m edge on the floor (the edge 'nearest' to you in Figures 2, 3 and 4), calculate:
   (a) the direct distance from Spike to Fred through the air;
   (b) the shortest distance over the walls and the floor or ceiling.

2   Measure the edges of your box and calculate the direct distance from Spike's corner to Fred's corner. Check by measurement.

3   Measure the length, width and height of your classroom or a room at home. Calculate the Spike–Fred direct distance.

4   A garage is 5 m long, 3 m wide, 3 m high. Can a 7 m pole be stored in it?

5

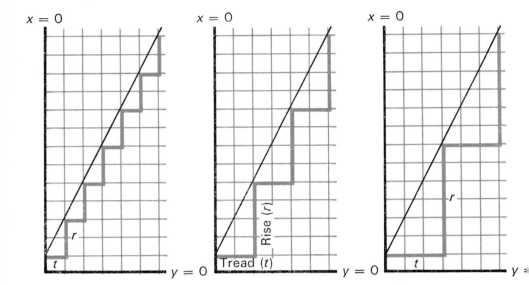

1. Gradients

1. GRADIENTS OF STRAIGHT LINE GRAPHS

1.1 Steepness of lines

In the drawing at the head of this chapter the line $y = 2x + 1$ has been drawn three times. A different 'staircase' has been drawn on the line each time. What is the value of $\dfrac{r}{t}$ for each of these staircases? This value is called the *gradient* of the line $y = 2x + 1$.

Clearly, in order to find the gradient of a line you do not need to fill in a full staircase. One stair would do.

By drawing suitable stairs, find the gradient of each of the lines in Figure 1.

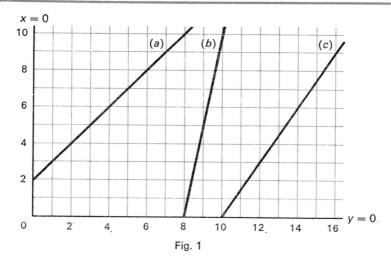

Fig. 1

Did you find that the steepest line had the largest gradient and that the least steep line had the smallest gradient?

Exercise A

For each of Questions 1–6, draw the line and find its gradient.

1   $y = 2x + 1$.   2 $y = x - 1$.

3   $y = 3x - 2$.   4 $y = \frac{1}{2}x + 4$.

5   $y = 4x - 3$.   6 $y = 4 + \frac{1}{3}x$.

7   Can you see the connection between the equation of a line and its gradient?

Write down the gradients of the next two lines without drawing them first.

(a) $y = 2x + 5$;   (b) $y = 8 + \frac{1}{4}x$.

8   Do you think that the following lines all have the same gradient?

$y = 2x + 1,$ $y = 2x,$ $y = 2 + 2x,$ $y = 2x - 1.$

Draw them all on the same diagram to see if you were right.

9   Find the gradient of the lines passing through:

(a) (1, 2) and (3, 6);   (b) (2, 3) and (4, 6);

(c) (0, 1) and (6, 4);   (d) (1, 1) and (3, 9).

1.2   Direction of slope

What is the gradient of line (a) in Figure 2?

What is the gradient of line (b)?

Did you give the same answer for both lines?

7

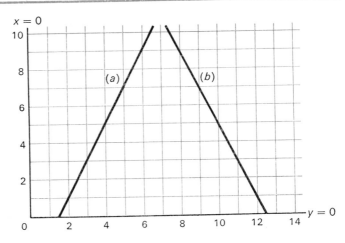

Fig. 2

The two lines do slope equally steeply, but in opposite directions, and it would be confusing if both were given the same gradient. To avoid this confusion we say that lines which slope from top left to bottom right (like line (*b*)) have negative gradients.

The gradient of line (*b*) is ⁻2 and the gradient of line (*a*) is ⁺2 or just 2. Figure 3 might help you to see the reason for this.

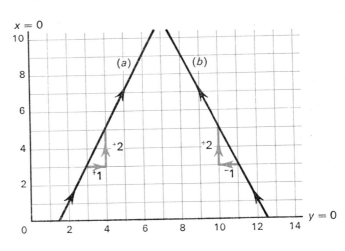

Fig. 3

Imagine an ant walking up each of the lines. For the 'stair' on line (*a*) it would go along 1 in the positive direction and up 2 in the positive direction.

$\dfrac{r}{t}$ is therefore $\dfrac{^+2}{^+1} = {}^+2.$

For the 'stair' on line (*b*) it would go along 1 in the negative direction and up 2 in the positive direction.

The value of $\dfrac{r}{t}$ is therefore $\dfrac{^+2}{^-1} = {}^-2.$

Exercise B

For each of Questions 1–6, draw the line and find its gradient.

1 $y = {}^{-}2x + 6$.
2 $y = {}^{-}x + 3$.

3 $y = {}^{-}\frac{1}{2}x + 2$.
4 $y = {}^{-}\frac{1}{3}x + 3$.

5 $y = 9 - 3x$.
6 $y = 12 - 4x$.

Write down the gradients of the lines in Questions 7–12.

7 $y = {}^{-}2x + 4$.
8 $y = 5 - 3x$.

9 $y = 5 - \frac{1}{2}x$.
10 $y = 2x + 3$.

11 $y = 4 + 3x$.
12 $y = 8 - 6x$.

13 Do the following lines all have the same gradient?

$y = 12 - 3x$, $y = 14 - 3x$, $y = {}^{-}3x + 9$, $y = 6 - 3x$.

Draw them all on the same diagram to see if you were right.

1.3 Finding gradients from the equation of a line

You should by now be able to spot immediately the gradient of a line like $y = 2x + 1$ or $y = 3 - 2x$.

Can you spot the gradient of $2y = 3x + 1$ or $3y + 2x = 12$?

Work through Exercise C and see if you can discover a method for writing down the gradient of any line without needing to draw the line.

Exercise C

1 What are the gradients of the two lines in Figure 4?

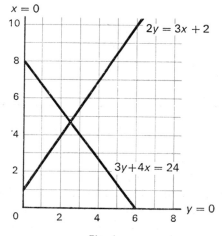

Fig. 4

2   For each part of this question, draw the line and measure its gradient.

    (a) $2y = 5x + 2$;   (b) $2y - 3x = 2$;

    (c) $3y - 2x = 1$;   (d) $4y + 3x = 24$.

3   Do the following lines all have the same gradient?

$$2y + 3x = 6,$$
$$2y + 3x = 12,$$
$$2y + 3x = 9,$$
$$2y + 3x = 24.$$

Draw them on one diagram to check your answer.

4   Have you found the rule for writing down the gradient of any line without needing to draw it? If you think you have, test it out with some examples of your own.

2. GRADIENTS OF GRAPHS WHICH GIVE SPECIAL INFORMATION

2.1 Travel graphs

Figure 5 shows the progress of a long distance runner who is training by running at a steady pace. The gradient of the graph gives us information about how fast he is running, but we must be careful because the scales on the two axes are different.

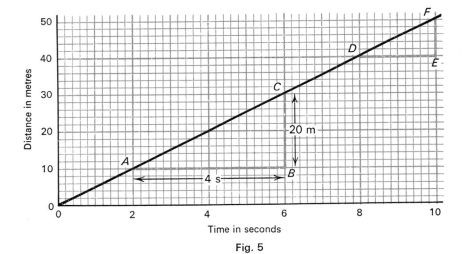

Fig. 5

Triangle ABC shows that the athlete ran 20 metres in 4 seconds, so he must have run 5 metres in 1 second. His speed of running is therefore 5 metres per second. We write this speed as 5 m/s.

Would you expect triangle DEF to give you the same answer for the speed? Check to make sure you are right.

Find the speeds at which people are travelling in the two graphs in Figure 6.

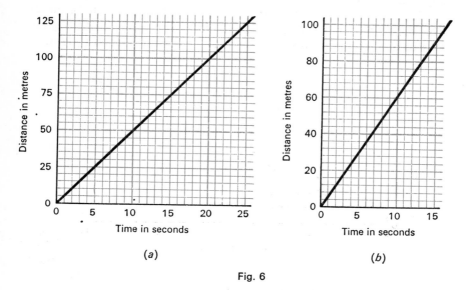

(a)   (b)

Fig. 6

What are the speeds during the three stages of the journey shown in Figure 7?

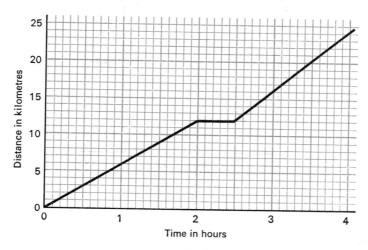

Fig. 7

2:2 Other gradients

Figure 8 shows the rate at which a bath was filled with water.

Triangle *ABC* shows that 4 litres of water ran into the bath in 8 seconds. This means that in 1 second $\frac{1}{2}$ litre ran in, so the gradient of the graph tells us that the bath is filling at the rate of $\frac{1}{2}$ litre per second ($\frac{1}{2}$ *l*/s).

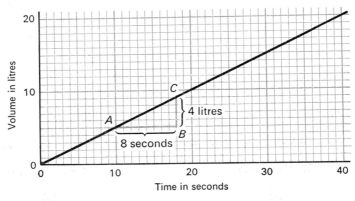

Fig. 8

What does the graph in Figure 9 show?
Using triangle *ABC*, find how many cards can be bought for 30p.
What is the cost per card?

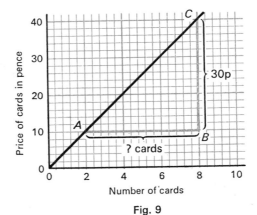

Fig. 9

Exercise D

1 In each of the graphs (*a*)–(*h*), describe what the graph shows and then work out the information given by the gradient. For example, in Figure 8 you would say that the graph shows how fast water runs into a bath and that the gradient shows that the bath fills at the rate of $\frac{1}{2}$ litre per second.

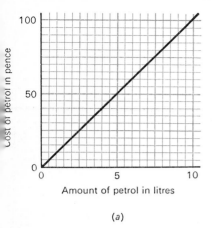

(a)

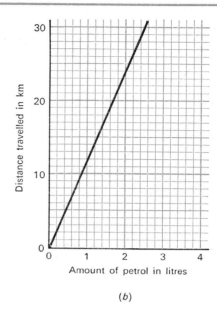

(b)

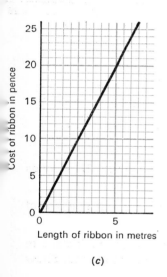

(c)

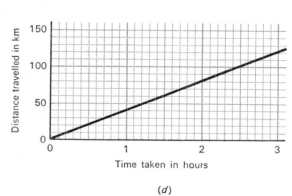

(d)

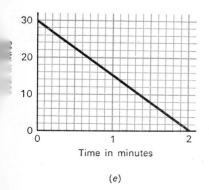

(e)

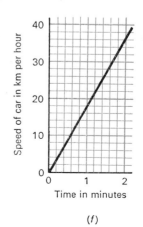

(f)

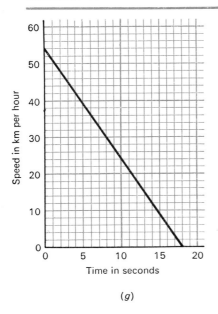

(g)

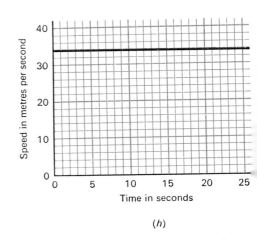

(h)

In Questions 2–7 draw the graph of each situation.

2   A boy running along a road at 6 metres per second.

3   A car travelling at 80 kilometres per hour for two hours.

4   A bath being filled at the rate of $\frac{2}{5}$ litre per second.

5   A car's petrol tank contains 1 litre of petrol. For the next 12 seconds petrol is added at the rate of $\frac{1}{2}$ litre per second.

6   A bath contains 30 litres of water. The water is run out at a rate of 2 litres per second until the bath is empty.

7   A car is stationary at traffic lights. The lights change and it starts to move. Its speed increases by 10 km per hour in each second. Show how its speed changes in the first 5 seconds.

3.   GRADIENTS OF HILLS

In geography lessons you may have discussed gradients of hills and mountains. You may also have seen notices saying things like 'Steep hill, gradient 1 in 4', or signs looking like Figure 10.

Fig. 10

Gradient 1 in 4 means the same as gradient $\frac{1}{4}$.
The slope AC in Figure 11 has a gradient of 1 in 4.

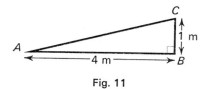

Fig. 11

Draw accurately a slope of 1 in 6.
Is a slope of 1 in 10 steeper or less steep than a slope of 1 in 4?
What do you think a gradient of 2 in 1 looks like? Draw an accurate diagram to show this. Where might you encounter a gradient like this?
Ordnance Survey maps have a special sign to show roads which are steeper than a certain gradient. Find out what this gradient is.
In practice, geographers have a slightly different method of measuring gradients to the one used by mathematicians. They would say that the slope AC in Figure 12 has a gradient of 1 in 4.

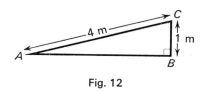

Fig. 12

Can you see how this differs from the gradient measured in Figure 11?
What practical advantage does the second method have?
Is there much difference between the two methods for most roads?
Draw diagrams to show slopes of 1 in 10, using each of the two methods.

4. ANGLES AND GRADIENTS

Use a protractor to draw an angle of 40° as shown in Figure 13.

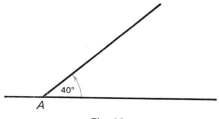

Fig. 13

Mark a point, *B*, 10 cm from *A* and use a protractor to draw a line *BC* at right-angles to *AB*.

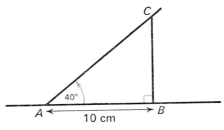

Fig. 14

Measure the length of *BC*.
Divide this length by 10 in order to find the gradient of *AC*.
Repeat for angles of 10°, 20°, 30°, 50°, 60°, 70° and 80°. Copy and complete this table:

Angle	Gradient
10°	
20°	
30°	
40°	
50°	
60°	
70°	
80°	

You can check your results by turning to the first page of Chapter 3.
You should have found that the gradient of a line at 40° was approximately 0·84. This means that for every 1 cm across the page, the distance up the page is 0·84 cm. See Figure 15.

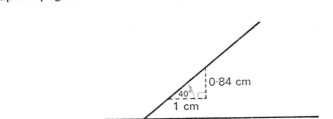

Fig. 15

For 2 cm across the page, the distance up would be 2×0.84 cm, that is, 1·68 cm (see Figure 16). The triangle is just a two times enlargement of the triangle in Figure 15.

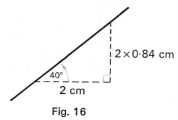

Fig. 16

What would be the distance up the page for a distance of 3 cm across the page?

Exercise E

For these questions use the table of gradients which you worked out.

1 Find the distances indicated by letters in Figure 17.

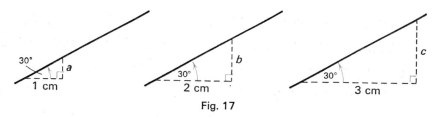

Fig. 17

2 Find the distances indicated by letters in Figure 18.

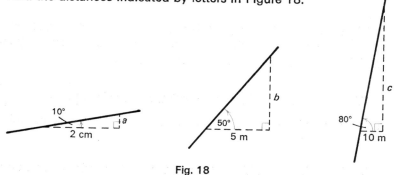

Fig. 18

3 A hill slopes upwards at 20° to the horizontal. How far would you rise vertically in travelling 1 metre horizontally?

How far would you rise in travelling 100 metres horizontally?

4 The gradient of a mountain slope is 2. Use your table of gradients to estimate its angle of slope.

5 What can be said about the gradient of lines sloping at (*a*) 0°, (*b*) 90° to the horizontal?

17

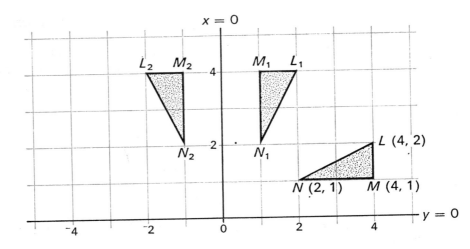

2. Combined transformations

(a) Draw triangle LMN with vertices at L (4, 2), M (4, 1) and N (2, 1). Transform triangle LMN by the matrix $\begin{pmatrix} 0 & 1 \\ 1 & 0 \end{pmatrix}$ and label the image $L_1 M_1 N_1$. What transformation does this matrix represent?

Now transform $L_1 M_1 N_1$ by the matrix $\begin{pmatrix} -1 & 0 \\ 0 & 1 \end{pmatrix}$ and label the new image $L_2 M_2 N_2$. What transformation does this matrix represent?
What single transformation would map LMN onto $L_2 M_2 N_2$?

The diagram at the head of this chapter shows that the first transformation followed by the second transformation has the same effect as an anticlockwise rotation of 90° about the origin.

We shall now try to find out whether the matrices $\begin{pmatrix} 0 & 1 \\ 1 & 0 \end{pmatrix}$ and $\begin{pmatrix} -1 & 0 \\ 0 & 1 \end{pmatrix}$ can be combined to give the matrix which represents this single transformation.

We know how to add, subtract and multiply matrices. Which operation do you think is most likely to be helpful?

Work out (i) $\begin{pmatrix} 0 & 1 \\ 1 & 0 \end{pmatrix} \begin{pmatrix} -1 & 0 \\ 0 & 1 \end{pmatrix}$; (ii) $\begin{pmatrix} -1 & 0 \\ 0 & 1 \end{pmatrix} \begin{pmatrix} 0 & 1 \\ 1 & 0 \end{pmatrix}$.

Draw diagrams to show the effect on triangle LMN of each of the resulting matrices. Do either of them represent an anticlockwise rotation of 90° about the origin? If so, which one?

(b) Transform the square in Figure 1 by the matrix $\begin{pmatrix} 2 & 1 \\ 0 & 1 \end{pmatrix}$ and label the image $P_1Q_1R_1S_1$.

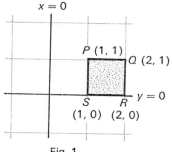

Fig. 1

Now transform $P_1Q_1R_1S_1$ by the matrix $\begin{pmatrix} -1 & 1 \\ 1 & 2 \end{pmatrix}$ and label the new image $P_2Q_2R_2S_2$.

Work out $\begin{pmatrix} -1 & 1 \\ 1 & 2 \end{pmatrix}\begin{pmatrix} 2 & 1 \\ 0 & 1 \end{pmatrix}$ to obtain a new matrix. Draw a diagram to show the effect of this new matrix on $PQRS$. What do you notice?

(c) Transform the square in Figure 1 by the matrix $\begin{pmatrix} -1 & 1 \\ 1 & 2 \end{pmatrix}$.

Now transform the image by the matrix $\begin{pmatrix} 2 & 1 \\ 0 & 1 \end{pmatrix}$.

What single matrix do you think would take the original square to the final shape? Check to see whether you are right.

(d) Compare your answers to (b) and (c). Does the order of the transformations make any difference to the final shape?

Exercise

1 Start with the square in Figure 1. Transform it by $\begin{pmatrix} 1 & 1 \\ -1 & 2 \end{pmatrix}$ and then transform the new shape by $\begin{pmatrix} 1 & 1 \\ 0 & 1 \end{pmatrix}$.

Work out $\begin{pmatrix} 1 & 1 \\ 0 & 1 \end{pmatrix}\begin{pmatrix} 1 & 1 \\ -1 & 2 \end{pmatrix}$ to obtain a new matrix. What is the effect of this new matrix on the original square?

2 Transform the square in Figure 1 by $\begin{pmatrix} 1 & 1 \\ 0 & 1 \end{pmatrix}$ and then transform the new shape by $\begin{pmatrix} 1 & 1 \\ -1 & 2 \end{pmatrix}$.

By multiplying two matrices together, find the matrix which takes the original square to the final shape.

Compare the final shape with the one which you obtained in Question 1. What can you say about the order of the transformations represented by $\begin{pmatrix} 1 & 1 \\ -1 & 2 \end{pmatrix}$ and $\begin{pmatrix} 1 & 1 \\ 0 & 1 \end{pmatrix}$?

3   (a) Start with the square in Figure 1. Transform it by $\begin{pmatrix} 2 & 0 \\ 0 & 1 \end{pmatrix}$ and then transform the new shape by $\begin{pmatrix} 1 & 0 \\ 0 & 2 \end{pmatrix}$.

     (b) Describe the transformations which $\begin{pmatrix} 2 & 0 \\ 0 & 1 \end{pmatrix}$ and $\begin{pmatrix} 1 & 0 \\ 0 & 2 \end{pmatrix}$ represent.

     (c) What single transformation would map the original square onto the final shape?

     (d) By multiplying two matrices together, find the matrix which represents this single transformation.

     (e) Would it make any difference to the final shape if you first transformed the square by $\begin{pmatrix} 1 & 0 \\ 0 & 2 \end{pmatrix}$ and then transformed the new shape by $\begin{pmatrix} 2 & 0 \\ 0 & 1 \end{pmatrix}$?

4   (a) Transform the quadrilateral in Figure 2 by $\begin{pmatrix} 2 & 0 \\ 0 & 2 \end{pmatrix}$ and then transform the new quadrilateral by $\begin{pmatrix} -2 & 0 \\ 0 & -2 \end{pmatrix}$.

     (b) Describe the transformations which $\begin{pmatrix} 2 & 0 \\ 0 & 2 \end{pmatrix}$ and $\begin{pmatrix} -2 & 0 \\ 0 & -2 \end{pmatrix}$ represent.

     (c) What single transformation would map the original quadrilateral onto the final quadrilateral? Find the matrix which represents this transformation.

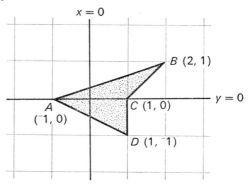

Fig. 2

5   (a) The matrix $\begin{pmatrix} 1 & 0 \\ 0 & 2 \end{pmatrix}$ represents a one-way stretch from the line $y = 0$ with stretch factor 2. What does $\begin{pmatrix} 1 & 0 \\ 0 & 3 \end{pmatrix}$ represent?

     (b) Work out $\begin{pmatrix} 1 & 0 \\ 0 & 2 \end{pmatrix}\begin{pmatrix} 1 & 0 \\ 0 & 3 \end{pmatrix}$. What does this new matrix represent? What is the combination of two one-way stretches from the line $y = 0$?

3. Trigonometry

1. GRADIENTS

In the chapter called 'Gradients' you drew lines at various angles and measured their gradients. Your results should have been something like this:

Angle	Gradient
10°	0·18
20°	0·36
30°	0·58
40°	0·84
50°	1·19
60°	1·73
70°	2·75
80°	5·67

(a) From the table it can be seen that the gradient of a hill sloping at 30° to the horizontal is 0·58. This means that for every 1 metre horizontally the distance up is 0·58 metres. See Figure 1.

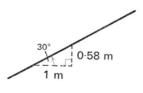

Fig. 1

For 2 metres horizontally, the distance up is $2 \times 0{\cdot}58$ metres, that is $1{\cdot}16$ metres. See Figure 2.

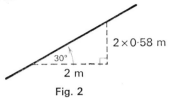

Fig. 2

What would be the distance up for 5 m horizontally?

(*b*) A ladder leans against a wall and makes an angle of 50° with the horizontal. The foot of the ladder is 4 metres from the wall. See Figure 3.

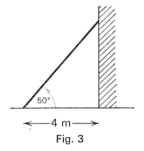

Fig. 3

The gradient table can be used to find how far up the wall the ladder will reach. The information shown in Figure 4 was obtained by looking up 50° in the table.

1·19 m
50°
1 m

Fig. 4

What enlargement would map Figure 4 onto Figure 3? Hence find the distance which the ladder reaches up the wall.

Exercise A

1   Find the distances indicated by letters in Figure 5.

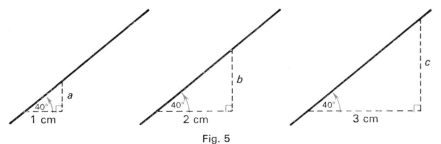

Fig. 5

22

2 Find the distance *a* in Figure 6.

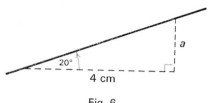

Fig. 6

3 A ladder leans against a wall and makes an angle of 70° with the horizontal. The foot of the ladder is 3 metres from the wall. How far up the wall does the ladder reach?

4 A hill slopes upwards at 20° to the horizontal. What is the gain in height in travelling 15 m horizontally?

5 Figure 7 shows a wire supporting a flagpole. The wire makes an angle of 60° with the horizontal and is fixed 8 m from the base of the flagpole. What is the height of the flagpole?

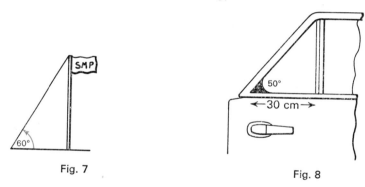

Fig. 7

Fig. 8

6 Figure 8 shows a triangular window of a car door. Calculate the height of the window.

2. TANGENTS

(*a*) The table on p. 21 gave the gradients of lines at angles of 10°, 20°, 30°, 40°, 50°, 60°, 70°, 80°. It might be necessary to know the gradient of lines at other angles, for example 35·2°. This information can be obtained from a book such as the S.M.P. *Elementary Tables*. You will find it under the name of *tangents*.

These tables can be used in the same way as the tables of sines and cosines. For example, the gradient of a line at 35° is obtained by finding 35 down the left-hand side, and looking in the column headed 0·0. You should get 0·700.

23

The gradient of a line at 35·2° is obtained by finding 35 down the left-hand side, and looking in the column headed 0·2. Check that you get 0·705.

You will remember that sine and cosine are abbreviated to sin and cos. Similarly, tangent is abbreviated to *tan*:

$$\tan 35° = 0·700,$$
$$\tan 35·2° = 0·705.$$

(*b*) A railway track slopes at 12·5° to the horizontal. To find its gradient look up 12·5° in your tangent tables.

Check that you agree that tan 12·5° is 0·222.

This means that for every 1 m horizontally the track rises by 0·222 m vertically (see Figure 9).

How far up would you go for 10 m horizontally?

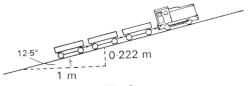

12·5°   0·222 m
1 m

Fig. 9

(*c*) The tangent tables can also be used the other way round. For example, if the gradient of a road is 0·184, its angle of slope can be found by looking up 0·184 in the body of the tangent tables.

Check that you get 10·4°.

Exercise B

1 Use your tables to find:

(*a*) tan 26·4°;   (*b*) tan 2·8°;   (*c*) tan 84·7°.

2 Use your tables to find the angles which have the following tangents:

(*a*) 0·360;   (*b*) 2·00;   (*c*) 1·00;   (*d*) 115.

3 A hill slopes at 23·6° to the horizontal. What is its gradient? How far up would you go for 10 m horizontally?

4 A railway track has a gradient of 0·080. What is its angle of slope?

5 Figure 10 shows a road sign. What is the angle of slope of the hill?

1 : 10

Fig. 10

3. USING TANGENTS

(a) Figure 11 shows a line passing through two points *A* and *B*. *A* has coordinates (1, 1) and *B* has coordinates (5, 4). The 'stair' from *A* to *B* is 4 along in the positive direction and 3 up in the positive direction. The gradient of the line is therefore $\frac{3}{4}$, that is, 0·75.

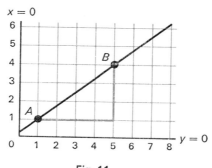

Fig. 11

The angle which *AB* makes with the line $y = 0$ can be found by looking up 0·75 in the tangent tables.

The numbers in the tables are given to 3 significant figures. This means that we must look for 0·750. Can you find it?

The nearest you can get is 0·751. This is the tangent of 36·9°.

The line in Figure 11 therefore makes an angle of just less than 36·9° with the line $y = 0$.

(b) A surveyor stands 40 m from a building and measures the *angle of elevation* of the top, that is, the angle from the horizontal up to the top of the building. He finds that it is 52·8°. The height of the measuring instrument above the ground is 1·5 m (see Figure 12).

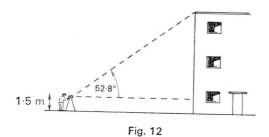

Fig. 12

We can use tangent tables to find the height of the building. By looking up 52·8° in the tables we get the information in Figure 13.

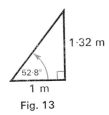

Fig. 13

Using a scale factor of 40, the height of the building above the measuring instrument is 40 × 1·32 m. Work this out.

Add on 1·5 m to find the height of the building above ground level.

Exercise C

1 A line passes through the points with coordinates (1, 2) and (3, 6). What is its gradient? Find the angle it makes with the line $y = 0$.

2 What is the angle of elevation of a building 50 m high from a point 200 m away?

3 Two posts are level with one another on opposite banks of a river. From a point on the bank 20 m away from one post, the angle between the directions of the posts is 32° (see Figure 14). What is the width of the river?

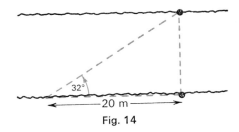

Fig. 14

4 A surveyor standing 80 m from a factory chimney measures the angle of elevation of the top as 35°. What is its height if the measuring instrument is 1·5 m above the ground?

5 A lean-to shed has a height of 2 m at the front and 4 m at the back, and is 5 m wide (see Figure 15). Find the angle of slope of the roof.

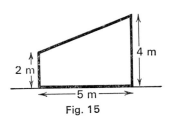

Fig. 15

4. MORE ABOUT TANGENTS

(*a*) You may wonder why the word tangent is used in connection with gradients.

The more familiar use of tangent refers to a line which just touches a curve (see Figure 16). What does the expression 'going off at a tangent' mean?

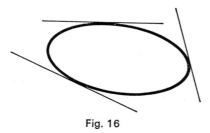

Fig. 16

Figure 17 shows a circle of radius 1 unit. The tangent at *A* has been drawn. The distance *AB* measured along this *tangent* line would tell us the gradient of *CB*. It was for this reason that the table of gradients became known as a table of *tangents*.

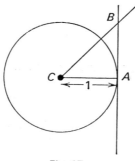

Fig. 17

(*b*) A window cleaner's ladder makes an angle of 22° with a wall when it just reaches a window 12 m up (see Figure 18). The problem is to find how far the foot of the ladder is from the wall.

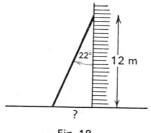

Fig. 18

In the previous work we have arranged for our basic triangle to be as shown in Figure 19.

Fig. 19

To get Figure 18 into this position it is necessary to reflect and rotate it. The simplest way to do this is to hold the page up to the light, rotate it through 90°, and look at it from the other side. The triangle will then appear as in Figure 20.

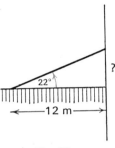

Fig. 20

Now looking up 22° in the tangent tables gives the information in Figure 21.

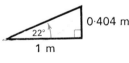

Fig. 21

What scale factor is needed to map Figure 21 onto Figure 20? Use this to find the distance indicated by the question mark in Figure 18.

(*c*) Figure 22 shows a triangle *ABC* with *AC* of length 1 unit.

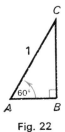

Fig. 22

The lengths of the other sides are sin 60° units and cos 60° units. See Figure 23.

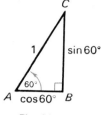

Fig. 23

The gradient of *AC* is therefore $\dfrac{\sin 60°}{\cos 60°}$.

But this is what we have called tan 60°.

This means that $\tan 60° = \dfrac{\sin 60°}{\cos 60°}$.

Check that this is so, by looking up 60° in your sine and cosine tables and working out $\dfrac{\sin 60°}{\cos 60°}$.

Choose any angle. Look up its sine and its cosine. Use your slide rule to divide the sine by the cosine. Check that this is the same as the tangent of the angle. (There may be a slight inaccuracy because the tables give only 3 significant figures.)

Exercise D

1 Find the lengths indicated by letters in Figure 24.

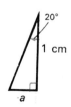 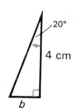 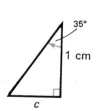 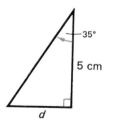

Fig. 24

2 Find the third angles of the triangles in Figure 25, and then use your tangent tables to find the lengths indicated by letters.

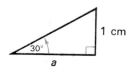 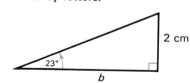

Fig. 25

2-2

3   A window cleaner's ladder makes an angle of 25° with a wall when it just reaches a window 10 m up (see Figure 26). How far is the foot of the ladder away from the building?

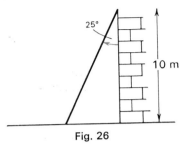

Fig. 26

4   A beam is supported by a stay-rod fixed to the wall 2 m below the beam and at 46° to the wall (see Figure 27). How far from the wall is the point of support on the beam?

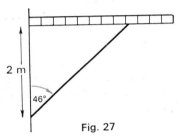

Fig. 27

5   A lamp, 12 m above the ground, sheds light in the shape of a cone (see Figure 28). Find the radius of the area illuminated on the ground.

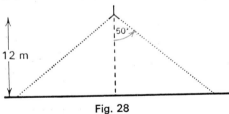

Fig. 28

6   The height of a pylon is 40 m (see Figure 29). If the angle of elevation of its top, measured from P, is 20°, what is angle b? Use this angle to find the distance of P from the centre of the base of the pylon.

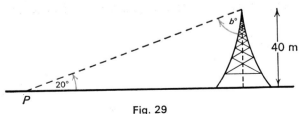

Fig. 29

7 How long is the shadow of a 20 m flagpole when the angle of elevation of the sun from the end of the shadow is 47°? See Figure 30.
(This angle is often called the *altitude* of the sun.)

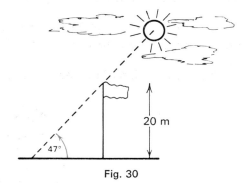

Fig. 30

8 From the top of a cliff 30 m high a boat is sighted at an angle of 20°
to the horizontal (see Figure 31). (This angle is often called the *angle
of depression.*) How far away is the boat from the cliff ?

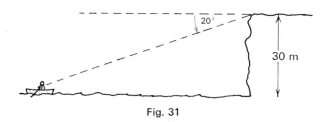

Fig. 31

5. MEASURING ANGLES

When a surveyor is measuring angles he uses a special instrument called
a theodolite. It is accurate, and expensive.
  It is possible to make a simpler and cheaper device for measuring angles
(see Figure 32).

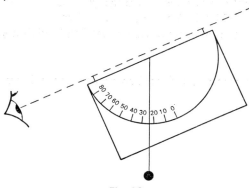

Fig. 32

On a piece of thick card or wood, mark out the angles using a protractor. Attach a piece of thread with a weight on the end as shown. You can also fix some 'sights' if you wish.

This device can be used for finding the heights of buildings and trees.

Suppose you want to find the height of a tree (see Figure 33). Stand a convenient distance from the trunk of the tree. Choose a distance like 10 m or 20 m.

Measure the angle of elevation of the top. Suppose it is 36°.

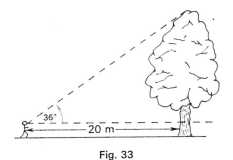

Fig. 33

From your tangent tables you would get the information shown in Figure 34.

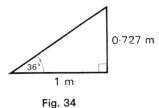

Fig. 34

The height of the top of the tree above your eye is therefore 20 × 0·727 m, that is, 14·54 m.

If the height of your eye above the ground is 1·5 m, then the height of the tree is (14·54 + 1·5) m, that is, 16·04 m.

Do you think that you would be justified in giving your answer to that accuracy?

Use the method just described to find the heights of some buildings and trees.

4. Areas under graphs

1. MOVING AT CONSTANT SPEED

1.1 Graphs with easy scales

Owen walks at 5 km per hour for 2 hours, then at 3 km per hour for 2 hours and then stops. How far has he walked?

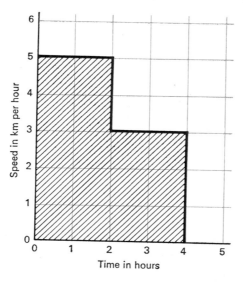

Fig. 1

Figure 1 is a graph showing Owen's speeds during his journey. How many squares are there in the shaded area? (This is called the area under the graph.)

The shaded area represents the distance Owen walked.

Exercise A

1   What are the distances travelled in each of the journeys shown in the graphs in Figure 2?

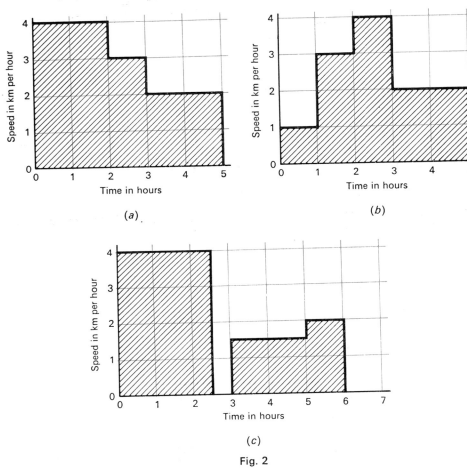

(a)

(b)

(c)

Fig. 2

2   A man training for a marathon runs for 2 hours at 13 km per hour and then for 1 hour at 10 km per hour and then for 1 hour at 9 km per hour.

(a) How far does he run?

(b) Draw a graph to show his speeds during the run, using the same scales as in Question 1. What distance does the area under the graph represent? Does this agree with your answer to part (a)?

1.2   Scales

In each of the graphs you have met so far, 1 square represented 1 km. Scales, however, are not always as simple as this.

Figure 3 represents a cyclist's journey. How fast was the cyclist travelling and for how long?

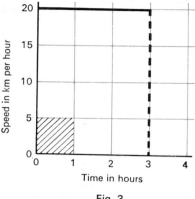

Fig. 3

The shaded square represents 5 km – make sure you understand why this is so.

How many squares of this size are under the graph? What distance is represented by the total area under the graph?

Is this what you would have expected?

Figure 4 shows a slightly different type of example:

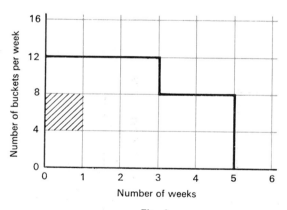

Fig. 4

The graph shows that the Grimes family used 12 buckets of coal per week for 3 weeks and then 8 buckets of coal per week for 2 weeks.

(*a*) How many buckets of coal did they use altogether?

(*b*) The shaded square represents a certain number of buckets of coal. How many?

(*c*) How many squares of this size are there under the graph?

(*d*) How many buckets of coal are represented by the total area under the graph? Does this agree with your answer to (*a*)?

Exercise B

1 For each of the graphs in Figure 5, first say what the shaded area represents and then what the total area under the graph represents.

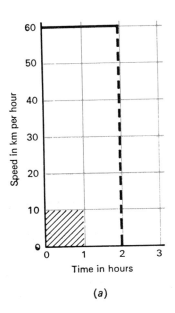

(a)

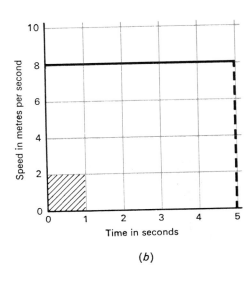

(b)

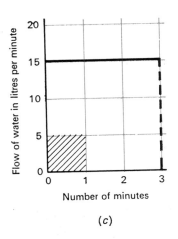

(c)

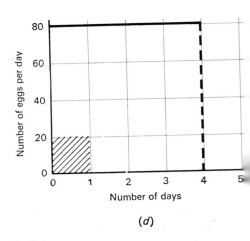

(d)

Fig. 5

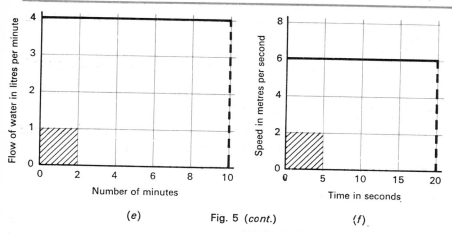

(e)　　　Fig. 5 (*cont.*)　　　(f)

2 What is the total amount of coal used in seven days (see Figure 6) ?

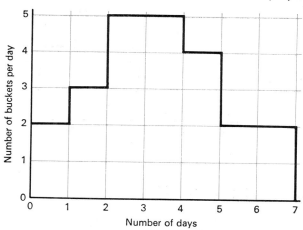

Fig. 6

3 Figure 7 shows a car journey.

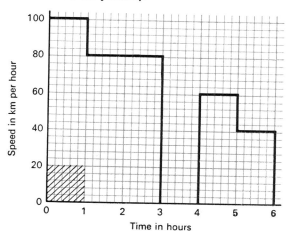

Fig. 7

(*a*) Describe the journey. (You might start : The car travels for 1 hour at 100 km per hour, then ....)

(*b*) What distance is represented by the shaded square ?

(*c*) What distance is represented by the total area under the graph ?

2. SPEEDING UP AND SLOWING DOWN

Look again at Figure 7. It is an unrealistic graph because no car could change instantly from 100 km per hour to 80 km per hour.

A more realistic graph might look like Figure 8.

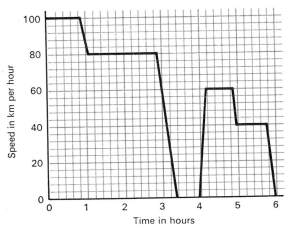

Fig. 8

What is happening in Figure 9 ?

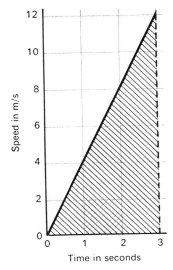

Fig. 9

This graph might show a sprinter getting up speed at the beginning of a race.

The double-shaded square represents 2 metres and nine of these squares would fit into the area under the graph. This means that the area under the graph represents 2×9 metres $= 18$ metres.

Does it seem reasonable that the sprinter covered 18 metres while speeding up?

He started at 0 metres per second, and, 3 seconds later, was moving at 12 metres per second.

If he had 'travelled' for 3 seconds at 0 metres per second, how far would he have gone?

If he had travelled for 3 seconds at 12 metres per second, how far would he have gone?

As he speeded up smoothly from 0 to 12 metres per second we might expect the distance to be half-way between 0 and 36 metres, which is 18 metres.

Exercise C

1 (*a*) What does the graph in Figure 10 show?

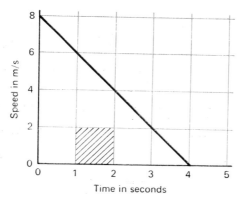

Fig. 10

(*b*) What does the shaded square represent?

(*c*) How many squares of this size are there under the graph?

(*d*) What does the total area under the graph represent?

2 For each of the graphs in Figure 11 (over page):

(*a*) Describe what they show and what the area under the graph represents.

(*b*) Work out the area under the graph. Remember to look at the scales carefully.

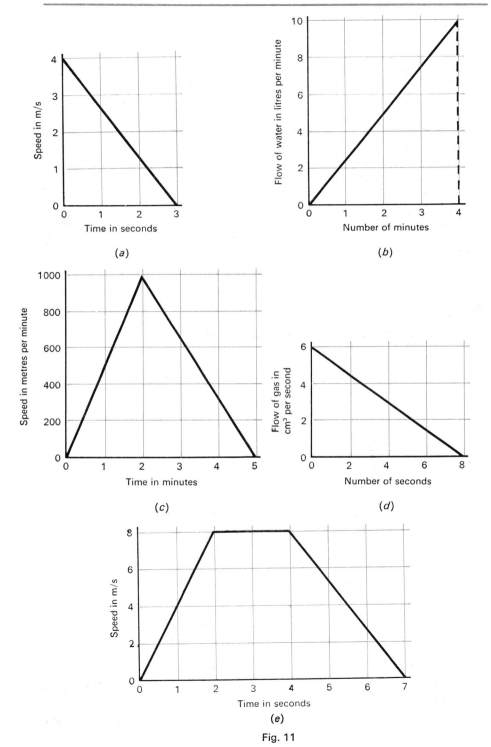

Fig. 11

3 The graph in Figure 12 shows a walk.

   (*a*) Describe the walk fully.

   (*b*) What is the total distance covered ?

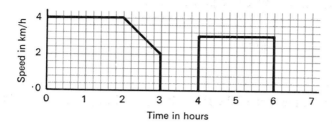

Fig. 12

3. IRREGULAR GRAPHS

Even the graphs in Section 2 are not very realistic, because drivers and walkers do not increase and decrease their speeds evenly. The graph of a car journey might look something like Figure 13.

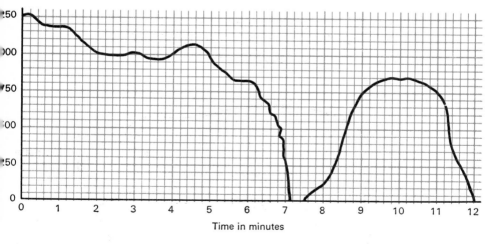

Fig. 13

The area under the graph would tell us the distance travelled by the car, but this area is quite difficult to find.

3.1 Finding irregular areas

In order to find the area of an irregular shape it is necessary to put the shape on to a square grid and then to count squares.

We will now have some practice at this.

Exercise D

1 Estimate the area of the shape in Figure 14 by putting it onto a square grid.

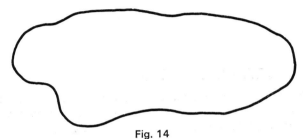

Fig. 14

2 Figure 15 is a scale drawing of an island.

(*a*) What area does the shaded square represent?

(*b*) What is the area of the island?

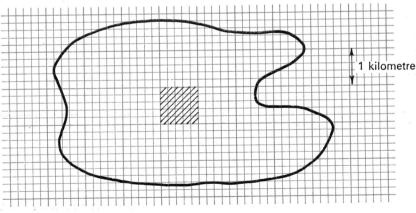

1 kilometre

Fig. 15

3 (*a*) What area does one shaded square represent on the scale drawing in Figure 16?

(*b*) What is the total area of this island?

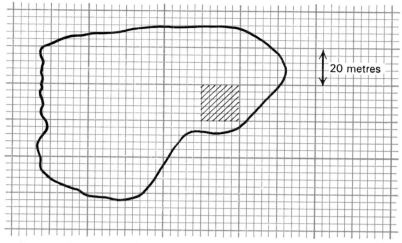

Fig. 16

3.2 More realistic graphs

The graph for a sprinter speeding up might be more like Figure 17.

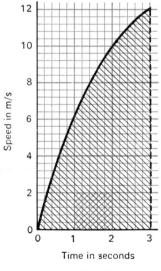

Fig. 17

The red square represents 2 metres. There are 8 complete squares of this size under the graph, so these represent 16 metres. In addition, there are approximately 80 small squares, which would make up $3\frac{1}{5}$ of the red squares and so represent $2 \times 3\frac{1}{5}$ metres $= 6\frac{2}{5}$ metres.

The total area under the graph is therefore approximately $22\frac{2}{5}$ metres. As this is only an approximate answer, it would be more sensible to say that the distance covered was 22 metres to the nearest metre.

Exercise E

1 Work out the distances covered in each of the graphs in Figure 18.

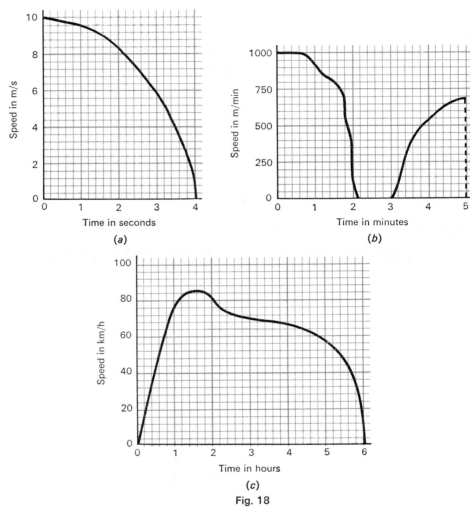

(a)

(b)

(c)

Fig. 18

2 This table gives the speeds of an engine pulling a heavy load at different times on a journey.

Time (in minutes)	0	1	2	3	4	5	6	7	8
Speed (in m/min)	0	30	80	150	250	350	490	590	630

(a) Plot these points on a graph and join them up as smoothly as possible.

(b) From the area under the graph find how far the engine travelled in 8 minutes.

3 Work out the distance travelled in the graph in Figure 13 on p. 41.

5. Statistics

1. THE MIDDLE HALF

We have seen how to answer the question:

'Is a mark of 56% above or below average?'

It is first necessary to decide which average is appropriate – the mean, mode or median – and then to find on which side of the central point the mark comes.

However, this information is not a great deal of use on its own. For example, do you think that a mark which is a little below average is very much worse than a mark which is a little above?

Look at Figure 1, the grouped frequency bar chart, which shows the results of an examination.

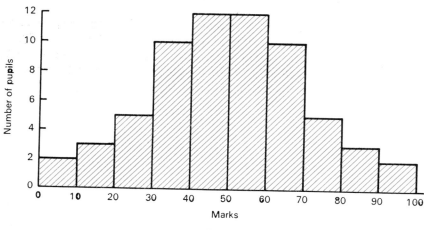

Fig. 1

The graph in Figure 2 shows the general shape of the distribution. The area under the graph is divided into three pieces by the dotted lines. Work out each of these areas. What do you notice?

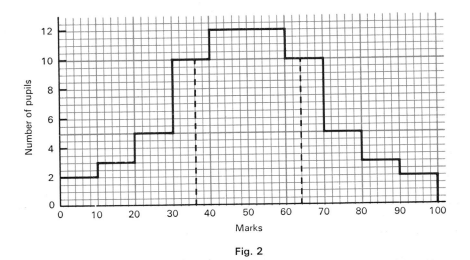

Fig. 2

Suppose that a teacher decides to give grades instead of marks for the examination, for example:

> A – good,
> B – satisfactory,
> C – weak.

He wants to grade half the class as satisfactory, one quarter as good and one quarter as weak.

You should be able to give the interval belonging to each grade just by looking at Figure 2, but can you tell just as easily how many pupils obtain each grade?

In *Book G* you found how to draw a cumulative frequency curve and this is the best form of graph to use for this problem (see Figure 3).

Copy this graph and draw the lines which show one quarter of the pupils graded as weak, one half of the pupils graded as satisfactory and one quarter graded as good. What is the interval for each grade?

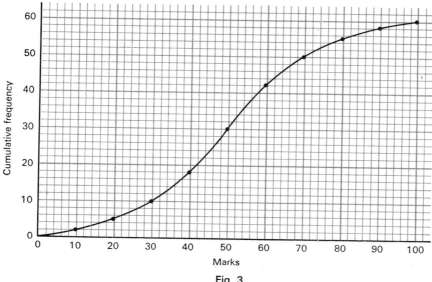

Fig. 3

2. QUARTILES

When a distribution is divided into four quarters, the quarters are called *quartiles*. Each quartile contains one quarter of the total population of the distribution. The numbers in the quarter and three-quarter positions are called the *lower quartile* and *upper quartile*, respectively.

The difference between the lower and upper quartiles is called the *inter-quartile range*. What is the inter-quartile range of the example just taken?

Perhaps a better question than 'Is a mark of 56% above or below average?' might be 'Is the mark between the upper and lower quartiles?' Why?

All this can be summarized by the diagram in Figure 4.

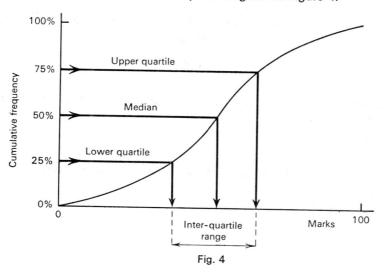

Fig. 4

47

Exercise A

1 Figure 5 shows the cumulative frequency graph of the results of an examination. From the graph state:

(*a*) the total number of pupils taking the examination;
(*b*) the median mark;
(*c*) the inter-quartile range;
(*d*) how many pupils scored 40 or less;
(*e*) how many pupils scored over 70 marks.

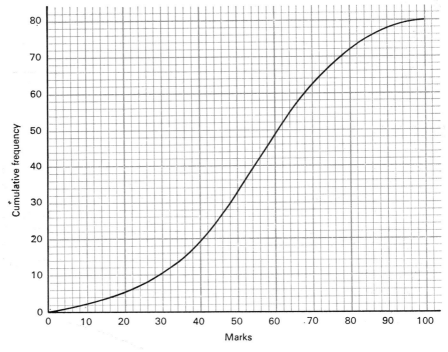

Fig. 5

2 Draw cumulative frequency curves for the pupils in your class showing:

(*a*) heights;
(*b*) weights;
(*c*) ages.

What is the median height, the median weight and the median age in each case?

Are you in the middle half?

3 The ages of 30 members of the 5th form at a school are grouped as follows:

Age (years and months)	15–5.2	15.3–15.4	15.5–15.6	15.7–15.8	15.9–15.10	15.11–16
Number of pupils	4	5	7	4	5	5

Make a cumulative frequency table for the ages of the form and draw a cumulative frequency curve. From your graph read off:

(a) the median age;
(b) the upper quartile;
(c) the lower quartile;
(d) the inter-quartile range.

How many pupils are younger than $15\frac{1}{4}$ years?

4 Explain the difference between the following two statements:

'Jean scored 50% in the last examination.'
'Jean's mark was the median mark in the last examination.'

5 A check was made on the speeds, measured to the nearest 10 km per hour, of 200 vehicles travelling along a road.

Speed (km per hour)	40	50	60	70	80	90	100	110	120
Frequency		1	4	9	14	38	47	51	32	4

Draw a cumulative frequency graph and use it to find:

(a) the median; (b) the inter-quartile range.

Use your graph to estimate the percentage of vehicles travelling:

(i) at less than 70 km per hour; (ii) at more than 110 km per hour.

6. Linear programming

4F decided to give a party and Peter volunteered to buy the Coca-Cola and sausage rolls for it. It was agreed that he should spend not more than £2 and that there should be at least twice as many sausage rolls as bottles of Coca-Cola. Bottles of Coca-Cola cost 8p each and sausage rolls 5p each. Can you work out how many sausage rolls and bottles of Coca-Cola he bought if he got as many bottles of Coca-Cola as possible?

Problems like this can take a long time to do by the trial and error method so we are going to learn a neater method for solving them. The method is called *linear programming*.

1. PROBLEMS WITH ONE CONDITION

We will first solve an easier problem than the one above.

Example 1

Jane's school has a drinks machine from which she can buy tea at 2 pence a cup and coffee at 3 pence a cup. Each week she spends a maximum of 24 pence on tea and coffee. In how many different ways can she do this?

We first write the information in the question as an algebraic expression. If Jane buys t cups of tea and c cups of coffee she will spend

$$2t + 3c \text{ pence.}$$

As she spends not more than 24 pence we know that:

$$2t + 3c \leqslant 24.$$

We now represent this information on a graph by drawing the line with equation $2t + 3c = 24$ and shading out the area we do not want (see Figure 1).

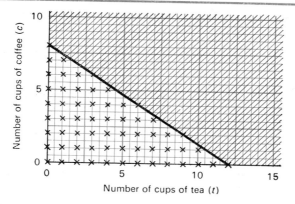

Fig. 1

Any points with whole number coordinates on or below the line belong to the solution set, and these points have been marked with crosses.

In how many ways could Jane spend 24 pence or less?

In how many of these ways would she spend exactly 24 pence? Where are the points which represent these ways?

One week Jane decided that she would spend less than 24 pence. In how many ways is this possible?

In this case we have $2t + 3c < 24$. The diagram for this would look just like Figure 1, except that the points on the line would not be marked.

Exercise A

1 John spends not more than 18 pence a week on tea at 2 pence a cup and coffee at 3 pence a cup.

(*a*) If he buys *t* cups of tea and *c* cups of coffee, copy and complete this expression:
$$2t + \qquad \leqslant 18.$$

(*b*) Draw a diagram to illustrate this relation, marking all the possible solutions with crosses.

(*c*) If he decides to spend less than 18 pence, which points marked on the diagram for part (*b*) will not count?

2 Robert was given this problem to solve: 'In a game, drawing a red counter scores 3 points and drawing a blue counter scores 4 points. Show graphically the ways of scoring less than 12 points.'

(*a*) He first wrote down the relation:
$$3r + 4b < 12.$$

Explain clearly what the letters *r* and *b* stand for.

(*b*) Draw a graph of the solution set.

3 Heather wants to score more than 24 points in the game described in Question 2.

(*a*) If she takes *r* red counters and *b* blue counters, copy and complete the expression:
$$3r + \quad > 24.$$

(*b*) Draw a diagram to show this situation. Can you mark all the possible solutions?

(*c*) How can she score more than 24 with the smallest number of counters?

4 A party of 30 people is to go out in 5-seater and 6-seater taxis. It does not matter if there are some spare seats, but no-one must be left behind. Let there be *f* 5-seater taxis and *s* 6-seater taxis, and copy and complete this expression:
$$\geqslant 30.$$

Draw a graph to show the possible ways in which the people might travel. Can you put a cross on each possible point? Explain your answer.

5 Daffodils cost 6 pence a bunch and tulips cost 8 pence a bunch. Sylvia wants to spend not more than 48 pence on daffodils and tulips.

(*a*) If she buys *d* bunches of daffodils and *t* bunches of tulips, write down an expression which must be true.

(*b*) Draw a graph to show the solution set.

(*c*) Which solution gives her the maximum possible number of bunches of tulips?

6 Look back at the problem at the beginning of this chapter. If Peter buys *b* bottles of Coca-Cola and *s* sausage rolls, write down the relation which shows that he must spend not more than £2.

Draw a graph to show this relation.

Use your graph to find the maximum number of bottles of Coca-Cola which can be bought. Does this also fit the condition that there must be at least twice as many sausage rolls as bottles of Coca-Cola?

If not, list some other pairs of solutions until you find a pair which fits both conditions.

2. PROBLEMS WITH TWO CONDITIONS

Example 2

Each week Jane spends a maximum of 24 pence on tea at 2 pence a cup and coffee at 3 pence a cup. She always buys a cup of tea at 11 a.m. from Monday to Friday, so she buys at least 5 cups of tea per week. Draw a graph of Jane's solution set.

We start exactly as in Example 1. If Jane buys t cups of tea and c cups of coffee:

$$2t + 3c \leqslant 24.$$

This gives the graph in Figure 1. Copy it, but do not mark the crosses.

We now have the extra condition that the number of cups of tea Jane buys is five or more. This can be written as:

$$t \geqslant 5.$$

On your copy of Figure 1, draw the line with equation $t = 5$, and shade out the region where t is less than 5.

All points in the unshaded region or on its boundaries are possible solutions to the problem. How many solutions are there?

Which gives the largest number of cups of coffee?

Check that your graph looks like Figure 2.

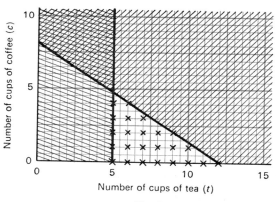

Fig. 2

Exercise B

1   Ben is asked to solve this problem: '30 people are to be taken out in 5-seater and 6-seater taxis. It does not matter if there are some empty seats. There is a maximum of two 6-seater taxis available, but plenty of 5-seater taxis. Draw a graph to show the solution set'.

(a) Ben first wrote down the relation:

$$5f + 6s \geqslant 30.$$

Explain fully what f and s stand for.

(b) Copy and complete the second relation he wrote down:

$$s \leqslant \quad .$$

(c) Draw a graph to show the solution set.

(d) Which ways use the smallest number of taxis?

(e) How many empty seats would there be if each of these combinations was used?

2 In a game, drawing a red counter scores 3 points and drawing a blue counter scores 4 points. There are many red counters but only three blue counters. John wants to score less than 24.

(*a*) If he takes *r* red counters and *b* blue counters, copy and complete these expressions:

$$< 24,$$
$$b \leqslant \quad .$$

(*b*) Draw a graph of the solution set. Be careful: the points on one boundary of your unshaded region will count, but not those on the other boundary.

3 A ferry has 12 vehicle spaces. A bus takes up 3 spaces and a car 1 space. There is always more than one bus on the ferry.

(*a*) If there are *b* buses and *c* cars, copy and complete these relations:

$$\leqslant 12.$$
$$b > \quad .$$

(*b*) Draw a graph to show the number of ways in which the spaces on the ferry can be partly or completely filled.

4 Joan has 18p to spend on cakes at 3p each and doughnuts at 2p each. She decides to buy not more than 4 cakes.

(*a*) If she buys *c* cakes and *d* doughnuts, write down the relation which shows that she spends 18 pence or less.

(*b*) What other condition, involving *c*, is given by the information in the question?

(*c*) Draw a graph to show Joan's possible purchases.

(*d*) Which way gives her the largest total number of cakes and doughnuts?

5 Susan has to make up bouquets of roses and carnations to present to the soloists after a concert. Roses cost 25p for a bunch of ten and carnations cost 40p for a bunch of ten. Susan has £2 to spend and wants to buy at least 2 bunches of carnations.

(*a*) Write down two relations which must be true, explaining carefully the meanings of the letters you use.

(*b*) Draw a graph of Susan's solution set.

(*c*) Write down the possibilities and say how she can buy the largest number of flowers.

6 In a small factory, product *X* gives £4 profit per article and product *Y* gives £5 profit per article. The factory can only make up to 35 of product *X* a week and up to 20 of product *Y* a week. It wants to make a profit of at least £200 a week.

(*a*) Write down three relations which must be true, explaining any letters you use.

(b) Draw a graph to show the solution set.

(c) Find the way or ways in which the factory can make a profit of over £200 by making as few as possible of product Y.

3. CONDITIONS LIKE 'AT LEAST TWICE AS MANY'

We must now learn to write information like 'there must be at least twice as many sausage rolls as bottles of Coca-Cola' as an algebraic expression.

3.1 Conditions like 'exactly twice as many'

Suppose first that Peter had to buy exactly twice as many sausage rolls as bottles of Coca-Cola. If b stands for the number of bottles of Coca-Cola and s for the number of sausage rolls, copy and complete this table of possible values of b and s:

b	s
2	4
3	
	10
	14
8	

You should notice that each line of your table fits the relation $s = 2b$ Look carefully at the relation. It is just a shorthand way of saying: 'The number of sausage rolls is equal to twice the number of bottles of Coca-Cola'.

Exercise C

1   David is told to buy exactly three times as many doughnuts as cakes. If he buys c cakes and d doughnuts, copy and complete this table of values of c and d:

c	d
1	3
2	
	12
	21
13	

Copy and complete the relation between c and d:

$$d = \quad .$$

2   A school has exactly half as many rugby players as soccer players. If there are r rugby players and s soccer players, copy and complete this relation:

$$r = \quad .$$

3 'There are exactly four times as many sparrows as blackbirds in that garden.' If there are *s* sparrows and *b* blackbirds, make out a table of possible values for *s* and *b*.
What is the algebraic relation connecting *s* and *b*?

3.2 Expressions like 'at least twice as many'

If the number of sausage rolls is at least twice the number of bottles of Coca-Cola, this table gives some possible values of *s* and *b*.

b	s
1	2 or 3 or 4 or 5 or ...
2	4 or 5 or 6 or 8 or 29 or ...
3	6 or 7 or 10 or ...

In each line, the value of *s* is equal to $2b$ or more than $2b$. So $s \geqslant 2b$.

Suppose David had been told to buy not more than 3 times as many doughnuts as cakes.
Copy and complete this table and then add some more values.

c	d
1	3 or 2 or 1 or ...
2	6 or 5 or or 3 or ...
3	9 or 8 or or ...
4	

Here, the value of *d* is exactly $3c$ or less than $3c$. So $d \leqslant 3c$.
If David had been told to buy less than 3 times as many doughnuts as cakes, which values would not be possible?
What would be the expression connecting *d* and *c* in this case?

Exercise D

1 A school has at least half as many rugby players as soccer players. If there are *r* rugby players and *s* soccer players, make out a table of possible values for *r* and *s*.
Copy and complete the relation connecting *r* and *s*:
$$r \geqslant .$$

2 'There are less than four times as many sparrows as blackbirds in that garden.' If there are *s* sparrows and *b* blackbirds, make out a table of possible values for *b* and *s*.
Write down the relation connecting *s* and *b*.

3 Frances is told to buy no more than three times as many buttons as pieces of ribbon. If she buys *b* buttons and *r* pieces of ribbon, copy and complete this relation:
$$b \leqslant .$$

4 A drama school always takes at least twice as many male students as female ones. If there are m male students and f female students, copy and complete this relation:

$$m \quad 2f.$$

5 In a rugby match there must be at least as many tries as conversions. If there are t tries and c conversions, write down the relation connecting t and c.

6 A school orchestra needs more than three times as many string players as wood-wind players. If there are s string players and w wood-wind players, write down the relation connecting s and w.

7 In planning an evening's television, it is decided that not more than twice as much time can be given to light entertainment as to current affairs. Write down a relation to describe this, explaining carefully what the letters you use stand for.

8 'There are always less than a third as many pupils taking French than there are taking mathematics in the 6th Form.' If m people take maths and f people take French, write down a table of possible values for m and f. What is the algebraic relation connecting m and f?

4. MORE PROBLEMS WITH TWO CONDITIONS

Example 3

A car park is to have s spaces for small cars and ℓ spaces for large cars. Each small space takes 2 sections of land and each large space 3 sections. 36 sections are available and there must be at least twice as many small spaces as large spaces. Find the possible combinations and state which will give space for most cars.

The two relations which must be true are:

$$2s + 3\ell \leqslant 36$$

$$\text{and} \qquad s \geqslant 2\ell.$$

Figure 3 shows the relation $2s + 3\ell \leqslant 36$. Copy it into your book.

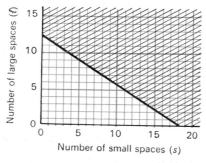

Fig. 3

On your copy of Figure 3, draw the line $s = 2\ell$. Check which side of this line gives values of $s > 2\ell$ and shade out the region which you do not want. Mark with a cross all the possible combinations. The points you have marked should include (10 small, 1 large), (9 small, 3 large) and (11 small, 4 large). If these are not included, you have made a mistake.

What is the largest number of car spaces which can be provided?

Exerise E

1 Gavin spends a maximum of 24p a week on tea at 2p a cup and coffee at 3p a cup. He buys less than half as much tea as coffee. If he buys *t* cups of tea and *c* cups of coffee:

(*a*) Write down the relation which shows that Gavin spends not more than 24p. Show this relation on a graph.

(*b*) Copy and complete the relation to show he buys less than half as much tea as coffee: $t < \quad .$

Show this relation on your graph.

(*c*) Mark all the possible solutions with a cross. Be careful: the points on one boundary of your unshaded region will not count.

(*d*) Which solutions give him the largest number of cups of tea?

2 Frances has 20p to spend on buttons at 1p each and pieces of ribbon at 2p each. She wants to buy at least three times as many buttons as pieces of ribbon.

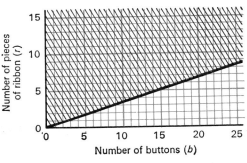

Fig. 4

(*a*) Figure 4 shows the condition that she buys at least three times as many buttons as pieces of ribbon. Write this information as an algebraic expression.

(*b*) Write the other information given in the question as an algebraic expression.

(*c*) Copy Figure 4 and show the second condition on your diagram.

(*d*) Describe the way, or ways, in which Frances can spend most of her money, while buying at least 3 pieces of ribbon.

3   Solve the problem about sausage rolls and Coca-Cola which was given at the beginning of this chapter. Your answers to Exercise A, Question 6 and the beginning of Section 3.2 will help you.

4   In a rugby match, the number of tries is always equal to or greater than the number of conversions. A team gained more than 24 points by scoring tries and conversions only. (A try gives 4 points and a conversion 2 points.)

   If the team scored t tries and c conversions:

   (*a*) Write down two relations which must be true.

   (*b*) Draw a diagram and find how the team could have scored more than 24 points with the smallest possible number of tries. There may be more than one possible answer.

5   Olive is knitting a football scarf for her boyfriend. It is to be made in red and white wool. Red wool costs 10p a ball and white wool 8p a ball, both balls being the same size. She cannot spend more than £1 and wants to have at least twice as much red as white in the scarf.

   (*a*) Write down two relations which must be true, explaining fully the meaning of any letters you use.

   (*b*) Draw a graph and find the largest possible number of balls she can buy. (There are four ways in which she can buy the greatest number of balls. What are they? Which one of them does not really fit the question?)

   (*c*) If Olive wanted exactly twice as much red as white, what would be the largest possible number of balls of wool?

6   A journalist receives £10 for a short article and £30 for a long article. He finds that he always sells less than half as many long articles as short ones. He needs to earn over £120 a month. Suppose he writes s short and ℓ long articles in a month:

   (*a*) Write down two relations which must be true.

   (*b*) Illustrate these two relations graphically and work out how he can earn the necessary money with the smallest amount of work if each short article takes him 4 hours to write and each long article takes 10 hours. (Be careful: will you count any points on the boundaries of the unshaded region?)

   (*c*) What is the smallest amount of work the journalist can do?

Review Chapters

7. Algebra

1. DIRECTED NUMBERS

Figures 1 (a) and 1 (b) should remind you of how to add directed numbers.

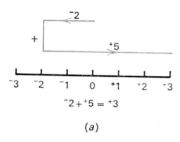

$^-2 + ^+5 = ^+3$

(a)

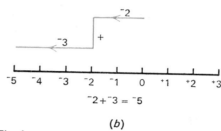

$^-2 + ^-3 = ^-5$

(b)

Fig. 1

Write down the answers to:

(a) $^+4 + ^-2$;　　(b) $^+2 + ^-4$;　　(c) $^-3 + ^+6$;　　(d) $^-2 + ^-3$.

1.1 Subtraction

Remember that:　(i) $^+5 - ^+3 = ^+5 + ^-3$,　　(ii) $^+5 - ^-3 = ^+5 + ^+3$.

Write down the answers to:

(a) $^+4 - ^+2$;　　(b) $^+2 - ^+4$;　　(c) $^+4 - ^-2$;　　(d) $^-4 - ^-2$.

1.2 Multiplication

This table should remind you of how to multiply directed numbers:

×	⁻3	⁻2	⁻1	0	⁺1	⁺2	⁺3
⁻3	⁺9	⁺6	⁺3	0	⁻3	⁻6	⁻9
⁻2	⁺6	⁺4	⁺2	0	⁻2	⁻4	⁻6
⁻1	⁺3	⁺2	⁺1	0	⁻1	⁻2	⁻3
0	0	0	0	0	0	0	0
⁺1	⁻3	⁻2	⁻1	0	⁺1	⁺2	⁺3
⁺2	⁻6	⁻4	⁻2	0	⁺2	⁺4	⁺6
⁺3	⁻9	⁻6	⁻3	0	⁺3	⁺6	⁺9

Notice the pattern of signs.

×	−	+
−	+	−
+	−	+

Write down the answers to:

(a) $^+3 \times ^-5$;　　(b) $^-2 \times ^+3$;　　(c) $^-2 \times ^-4$;　　(d) $^-\frac{1}{2} \times ^+6$.

1.3 Division

Since $^+5 \times ^-3 = ^-15$, it follows that $^-15 \div ^+5 = ^-3$.
Since $^-5 \times ^-3 = ^+15$, it follows that $^+15 \div ^-5 = ^-3$.
Write down the answers to:

  (a) $^+6 \div ^-2$;   (b) $^-8 \div ^+4$;   (c) $^-10 \div ^-5$;   (d) $^+3 \div ^-6$.

1.4 Mixed examples

Work out:

  (a) $^-3 + ^+5$;   (b) $^-3 \times ^+5$;   (c) $^+4 - ^-3$;   (d) $^+4 - ^+3$;
  (e) $^-8 \div ^+2$;   (f) $^-3 \div ^-6$;   (g) $^-2 - ^-8$;   (h) $^+2 + ^-7$.

2. MAPPING DIAGRAMS

2.1 With one operation

Figure 2 shows a mapping diagram for $x \to 2x$.

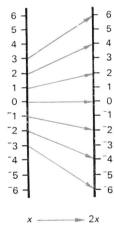

Fig. 2

Draw mapping diagrams for:

  (a) $x \to x+2$; (b) $x \to x-2$; (c) $x \to \frac{1}{2}x$; (d) $x \to ^-2x$.

Describe the pattern in each diagram.

2.2 With two operations

Figure 3 shows a mapping diagram for $x \to 2x+1$. We could use this mapping diagram to solve equations.

For example, if you wanted to solve the equation $2x+1 = 5$ you would start at 5 on the right-hand side (black arrow) and follow the red arrowed lines back to the left-hand side. What number would you reach?

Check that this gives the solution of $2x+1 = 5$.

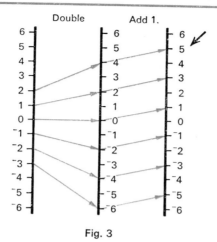

Fig. 3

(*a*) Use this method to solve the equations:

(i) $2x+1 = {}^-5$;   (ii) $2x+1 = {}^-1$.

The two parts of the mapping diagram for $x \to 2x+1$ could be combined to give Figure 4.

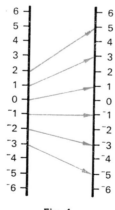

Fig. 4

(*b*) Draw mapping diagrams, like either that in Figure 3 or that in Figure 4, for:

(i) $x \to 3x-2$;   (ii) $x \to \frac{1}{2}x+3$;

(iii) $x \to 2(x-1)$;   (iv) $x \to x^2+1$.

(*c*) Use these mapping diagrams to solve the equations:

(i) $\frac{1}{2}x+3 = 2$;   (ii) $2(x-1) = 0$;

(iii) $3x-2 = {}^-5$;   (iv) $x^2+1 = 5$ (two answers).

3. INVERSE MAPPINGS

Figure 5 shows the mapping diagrams for $x \to 2x$ and its inverse, $x \to \frac{1}{2}x$.

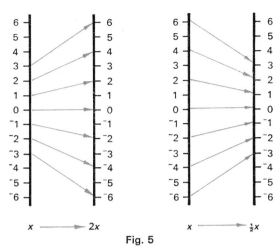

Fig. 5

Draw the mapping and inverse mapping diagrams for each of the following, labelling the inverse mappings.

(a) $x \to x - 1$;   (b) $x \to \frac{1}{3}x$;   (c) $x \to 3 - x$;   (d) $x \to \dfrac{12}{x}$.

What did you find happened in the last two examples?
What special name is given to mappings like these?

4. INVERSE OPERATIONS

The inverse operation for 'add 6' is 'take away 6'.
What is the inverse operation for 'take away 3'?
What is the inverse operation for 'multiply by 2'?
What is the inverse operation for 'divide by 5'?
What is the inverse operation for 'take away from 8'?
What is the inverse operation for 'divide into 12'?

5. EQUATIONS

5.1 Equations with no self-inverse operations

Figure 6 shows how to solve the equation $3x - 2 = 7$.

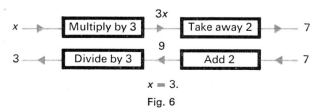

$x = 3.$

Fig. 6

Figure 7 shows part of the solution of the equation $2(x+2) = ^-4$. Complete the solution.

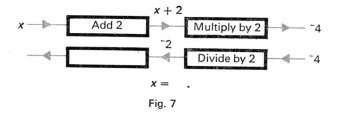

Fig. 7

Solve these equations:

(a) $4x-1 = 11$;   (b) $3(x-1) = 12$;   (c) $2x+5 = ^-1$;

(d) $2(x+3) = ^-8$;   (e) $2x+1 = ^-5$.

What is the connection between this method of solving equations and the one given in Section 2.2?

5.2 Equations with self-inverse operations

Figure 8 shows how to solve the equation $6-2x = ^-3$.

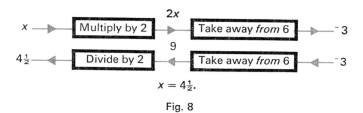

Fig. 8

Figure 9 shows part of the solution of the equation $12 - \dfrac{8}{x} = 10$.

Complete the solution.

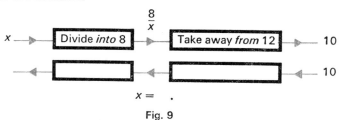

Fig. 9

Solve these equations:

(a) $8-x = ^-2$;

(b) $\dfrac{6}{x}+1 = 3$;

(c) $10-3x = ^-2$;

(d) $8-\dfrac{12}{x} = 2$.

5.3 More practice at equations

Work out the solutions to these equations:

(a) $^{-}2x+3 = 7$;   (b) $^{-}3(x-1) = 9$;

(c) $8-3x = {}^{-}1$;   (d) $4+\dfrac{6}{x} = 8$;

(e) $2(3x-1) = 10$;   (f) $3(6-2x) = 9$;

(g) $\frac{1}{2}(2x+5) = 3$;   (h) $\frac{1}{3}\left(\dfrac{8}{x}-2\right) = {}^{-}2$.

6. INVERSE ELEMENTS

The identity for addition is 0.
The inverse under addition for $^{+}2$ is $^{-}2$.
The inverse under addition for $^{-}3$ is $^{+}3$.

(a) What are the inverses under addition for:

    (i) $^{+}4$;   (ii) $^{-}2$;   (iii) $^{+}\frac{1}{2}$;   (iv) $^{-}\frac{2}{3}$?

(b) What is the identity for multiplication in the set of directed numbers?

(c) What are the inverses under multiplication for:

    (i) $^{+}3$;   (ii) $^{-}3$;   (iii) $\frac{1}{2}$;   (iv) $^{-}\frac{1}{3}$;   (v) $^{-}1$?

(d) Solve these equations by the method of inverse elements, showing all your working:

    (i) $3x = 5$;   (ii) $x+2 = {}^{-}3$;   (iii) $2x+3 = 7$;

    (iv) $3(x-2) = 9$;   (v) $3x-5 = {}^{-}8$;   (vi) $2(x+4) = {}^{-}6$;

    (vii) $6-x = 7$;   (viii) $8-3x = {}^{-}4$.

7. FORMULAS

7.1 Writing down formulas

'The time taken to cook a joint of meat is found by multiplying the weight of the joint (in kg) by 40 and adding on 30. The time is given in minutes'.
This sentence can be given by the formula:

$$T = 40W+30,$$

where T is the total time (in minutes) and W is the weight of the joint (in kg).

Write each of these sentences as a formula:

(a) The area of a rectangle is found by multiplying its length by its width.

(b) To find the area of a circle you first square the radius and then multiply by π.

(c) The sum of the angles of a polygon is found by taking away 2 from the number of sides of the polygon and then multiplying by 180.

7.2 Substitution into formulas

The main problem here is to remember in which order you should perform the operations. Work through the following three examples carefully:

(a) $A = 2(x+y)$. Find A if $x = 2$ and $y = {}^-4$.
$$A = 2(2+{}^-4)$$
$$= 2 \times {}^-2$$
$$= {}^-4.$$

Copy and complete Examples (b) and (c).

(b) $T = 3x^2$. Find T when $x = 4$.
$$T = 3 \times 4^2$$
$$= 3 \times$$
$$=$$

(c) $D = \dfrac{a+2b}{3c}$. Find D when $a = 22$, $b = {}^-2$ and $c = 2$.
$$D = \frac{22 + {}^-4}{6}$$
$$=$$

Work these out for yourself:

(d) $v = u + at$. Find v when $a = 10$, $u = 4$ and $t = 2$.
(e) $z = (3y)^2$. Find z when $y = 2$.
(f) $D = \dfrac{a+b}{c}$. Find D when $a = 6$, $b = {}^-4$ and $c = {}^-2$.
(g) $y = (x+1)^2$. Find y when $x = {}^-3$.

7.3 More substitution into formulas

$E = \frac{1}{2}mv^2$. Find m if $E = 54$ and $v = 3$.
$$54 = \tfrac{1}{2} \times m \times 9.$$
Can you now spot the value of m? If not, complete this flow diagram:

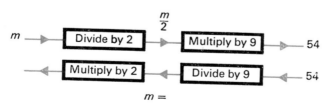

$$m =$$

Work these out for yourself:

(a) $C = 3d$. Find d if $C = 21$.
(b) $v = u + at$. Find u if $v = 34$, $a = 10$ and $t = 3$.
(c) $v = u + at$. Find a if $v = 30$, $u = 10$ and $t = 4$.
(d) $y = 2x^2$. Give two possible values of x if $y = 32$.

67

8. Number

1. FACTORS AND MULTIPLES

A factor is a counting number which divides a whole number of times into another counting number. For example, 6 is a member of the set of factors of 18 and we can write

$$6 \in \{\text{factors of } 18\}.$$

(*a*) Write down *all* the members of (i) {factors of 18}; (ii) {factors of 30}.

(Remember that 1 and 18 are factors of 18.)

(*b*) List the members of

$$\{\text{factors of } 18\} \cap \{\text{factors of } 30\},$$

that is, list the numbers which are factors of *both* 18 *and* 30.

Since 6 is a factor of 18, 18 is a multiple of 6, that is,

$$18 \in \{\text{multiples of } 6\}.$$

(*c*) Let $S = \{6, 12, 18, 24, \ldots\} = \{\text{multiples of } 6\}$

and $F = \{4, 8, 12, 16, \ldots\} = \{\text{multiples of } 4\}.$

Copy and complete the statement:

$$S \cap F = \{12, \ , \ , \ , \ldots\} = \{\text{multiples of} \quad\}.$$

A number greater than 1 which has only two factors, itself and 1, is called a *prime* number. So

$$\{\text{prime numbers}\} = \{2, 3, 5, 7, 11, 13, 17, 19, 23, 29, 31, 37, 41, \ldots\},$$

and $\{\text{prime factors of } 18\} = \{2, 3\}.$

Although there are only two prime factors of 18, we need to use the 3 twice in order to express 18 in prime factors:

$$18 = 2 \times 3 \times 3$$

or, in index form, $18 = 2 \times 3^2.$

(*d*) Write down all the factors of (i) 42; (ii) 27; (iii) 80.

(*e*) What are the prime factors of (i) 42; (ii) 27; (iii) 80?

(*f*) Express in prime factors (i) 42; (ii) 27; (iii) 80. Write your answers in index form.

2. FRACTIONS

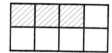

This rectangle is divided into 8 equal parts. We say that three-eighths ($\frac{3}{8}$)of the rectangle is shaded red.

The same portion of an object can be described by 'different-looking' fractions:

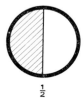 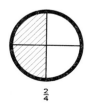  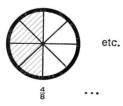

$\frac{1}{2}$ $\qquad$ $\frac{2}{4}$ $\qquad$ $\frac{3}{6}$ $\qquad$ $\frac{4}{8}$ $\quad$ ...

$\{\frac{1}{2}, \frac{2}{4}, \frac{3}{6}, \frac{4}{8}, ...\}$ is a set of *equivalent* fractions. Members of this set can be formed by multiplying the top and bottom of the first fraction by the same number. For example,

$$\frac{5 \times 1}{5 \times 2} = \frac{5}{10} \quad \text{and} \quad \frac{11 \times 1}{11 \times 2} = \frac{11}{22}$$

belong to the set.

(a) Write down two more members of the set.

(b) Write down four fractions which are equivalent to $\frac{5}{9}$.

(c) Copy and complete:

$\quad$ (i) $\frac{2}{5} = \frac{}{15}$; $\quad$ (ii) $\frac{7}{12} = \frac{35}{}$; $\quad$ (iii) $\frac{20}{55} = \frac{}{11}$; $\quad$ (iv) $\frac{21}{70} = \frac{3}{}$.

We can use equivalent fractions to help us to compare fractions and to add and subtract fractions. Copy and complete the following examples.

Example 1

$\quad$ Compare $\frac{3}{4}$ and $\frac{4}{5}$.

$$\frac{3}{4} = \frac{}{20} \quad \text{and} \quad \frac{4}{5} = \frac{}{20}.$$
$$\frac{15}{20} < \frac{16}{20} \quad \text{and so} \quad \frac{3}{4} \quad \frac{4}{5}.$$

Example 2

$\quad$ Work out $1\frac{2}{9} - \frac{5}{6}$.

$\quad\quad$ $1\frac{2}{9}$ is the same as $\frac{11}{9} = \frac{}{18}$ and $\frac{5}{6} = \frac{}{18}$.

Therefore $\quad\quad\quad\quad 1\frac{2}{9} - \frac{5}{6} = \frac{22}{18} - \frac{}{18} = \frac{}{18}.$

(*d*) Arrange in order of size, smallest first: $\frac{2}{3}, \frac{1}{2}, \frac{7}{10}, \frac{5}{6}, \frac{3}{5}$.

(*e*) Work out:

(i) $\frac{3}{8} + \frac{1}{3}$;　　　　(ii) $\frac{2}{3} - \frac{1}{2}$;　　　　(iii) $\frac{3}{7} - \frac{2}{5}$;

(iv) $\frac{4}{9} + \frac{2}{3}$;　　　　(v) $2\frac{3}{5} + 1\frac{2}{3}$;　　　　(vi) $3\frac{3}{8} - 1\frac{1}{6}$.

Now copy and complete the following examples of multiplication and division.

Example 3

Work out $\frac{3}{4} \times \frac{7}{10}$.

$$\frac{3}{4} \times \frac{7}{10} = \frac{3 \times 7}{4 \times 10} = \text{———}.$$

Example 4

Work out $\frac{2}{3} \div \frac{5}{7}$.

$$\frac{2}{3} \div \frac{5}{7} = \frac{\frac{2}{3}}{\frac{5}{7}} = \frac{\frac{2}{3} \times}{\frac{5}{7} \times \frac{7}{5}} = \frac{\frac{14}{15}}{1} = \frac{}{15}.$$

Why is it helpful to multiply the top and bottom numbers by $\frac{7}{5}$?

(*f*) Work out:

(i) $\frac{1}{3} \times \frac{2}{5}$;　　　　(ii) $\frac{5}{9} \times \frac{3}{10}$;　　　　(iii) $\frac{5}{8} \times 2\frac{2}{3}$;

(iv) $\frac{3}{5} \div \frac{7}{10}$;　　　　(v) $\frac{5}{8} \div 1\frac{1}{4}$;　　　　(vi) $2\frac{1}{2} \div \frac{5}{6}$.

3. DECIMALS

17·46 means $(1 \times 10) + (7 \times 1) + (4 \times \frac{1}{10}) + (6 \times \frac{1}{100})$.

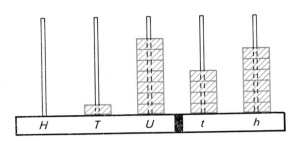

We add, subtract, multiply and divide with decimals in much the same way as we do with whole numbers:

$2\cdot47 + 0\cdot14$

$$\begin{array}{r} 2\cdot47 \\ +0\cdot14 \\ \hline 2\cdot61 \end{array}$$

$23\cdot1 - 1\cdot65$

$$\begin{array}{r} 23\cdot1 \\ -1\cdot65 \\ \hline 21\cdot45 \end{array}$$

$2 \cdot 63 \times 3 \cdot 7$	$2 \cdot 63 \times 3 \cdot 7$	263
	$= \dfrac{263 \times 37}{1000}$	$\times 37$
		7890
	$= 9 \cdot 731$	1841
		9731
$41 \cdot 23 \div 1 \cdot 9$	$\dfrac{41 \cdot 23}{1 \cdot 9}$	21·7
		19)412·3
	$= \dfrac{41 \cdot 23 \times 10}{1 \cdot 9 \times 10}$	38
		32
	$= \dfrac{412 \cdot 3}{19}$	19
		133
	$= 21 \cdot 7$	133

(*a*) Work out 29×42 and use your answer to write down the value of:

   (i) $2 \cdot 9 \times 4 \cdot 2$;   (ii) $0 \cdot 29 \times 420$;   (iii) $2 \cdot 9 \times 0 \cdot 0042$.

(*b*) Work out $861 \cdot 3 \div 27$ and use your answer to write down the value of:

   (i) $86 \cdot 13 \div 2 \cdot 7$;   (ii) $0 \cdot 8613 \div 27$;   (iii) $8 \cdot 613 \div 0 \cdot 027$.

(*c*) Find the *exact* value of:

   (i) $22 \cdot 7 \times 0 \cdot 38$;   (ii) $9 \cdot 916 \div 53 \cdot 6$.

4. NUMBER BASES

We can write numbers in bases other than ten.

214_{five} means $(2 \times 25) + (1 \times 5) + (4 \times 1)$, which is 59_{ten}.

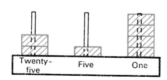

$101 \cdot 1_{\text{two}}$ means $(1 \times 4) + (0 \times 2) + (1 \times 1) + (1 \times \frac{1}{2})$, which is $5 \cdot 5_{\text{ten}}$.

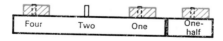

Remember that the largest digit we can use is one less than the number base in which we are working:

Number base	*Digits*
ten	0, 1, 2, 3, 4, 5, 6, 7, 8, 9.
nine	0, 1, 2, 3, 4, 5, 6, 7, 8.
eight	0, 1, 2, 3, 4, 5 6, 7.
etc.	

71

(*a*) What is the largest digit which we can use in base four?

(*b*) What digits can we use in base twelve? You will need to invent two new symbols. How would you write 142_{ten} in base twelve?

(*c*) What does the 3 mean in 31 if it is written in:

   (i) base ten;   (ii) base seven;   (iii) base four?

We can do arithmetic in bases other than ten. For example:

$$23_{five} + 34_{five} = 112_{five}$$

$$\begin{array}{r} 23 \\ +34 \\ \hline 112 \end{array}$$

$$61_{eight} - 47_{eight} = 12_{eight}$$

$$\begin{array}{r} 61 \\ -47 \\ \hline 12 \end{array}$$

$$1011_{two} \times 11_{two} = 100001_{two}$$

$$\begin{array}{r} 1011 \\ \times 11 \\ \hline 10110 \\ 1011 \\ \hline 100001 \end{array}$$

$$100001_{two} \div 11_{two} = 1011_{two}$$

$$\begin{array}{r} 1011 \\ 11\overline{)100001} \\ 11 \\ \hline 100 \\ 11 \\ \hline 11 \\ 11 \\ \hline \end{array}$$

(*d*) Work out:

   (i) $23_{six} + 45_{six}$;   (ii) $10111_{two} + 1101_{two}$;

   (iii) $83_{nine} - 64_{nine}$;   (iv) $1111_{two} \times 1001_{two}$;

   (v) $123_{four} \times 22_{four}$;   (vi) $100011_{two} \div 101_{two}$.

Write your answers in the given base.

5. TYPES OF DECIMAL

Some fractions can be written as terminating decimals, for example:

$$\tfrac{3}{4} = 0 \cdot 75$$

$$\begin{array}{r} 4\overline{)3 \cdot 00} \\ \hline 0 \cdot 75 \end{array}$$

and other fractions can be written as recurring decimals, for example:

$$\tfrac{2}{7} = 0 \cdot \dot{2}8571\dot{4}$$

$$\begin{array}{r} 7\overline{)2 \cdot 0000000\ldots} \\ \hline 0 \cdot 2857142\ldots \end{array}$$

(a) Write the following terminating decimals as fractions in their simplest form:

(i) 0·5; (ii) 2·8; (iii) 0·068.

(b) Write the following fractions as decimals:

(i) $\frac{5}{8}$; (ii) $\frac{2}{3}$; (iii) $\frac{5}{11}$.

There are decimals which neither terminate nor recur and which therefore cannot be written as fractions or ratios. Such numbers are called *irrational*.

(c) Which of the following numbers are irrational:

(i) $\sqrt{3}$; (ii) 3·7; (iii) $\sqrt{10}$; (iv) π; (v) $\sqrt{36}$?

6. SETS

When the members of one set A can all be found in another set B, then A is called a subset of B, and we write

$$A \subset B.$$

For example:

{pupils in your class} $\subset$ {pupils in your school};
{multiples of 4} $\subset$ {even numbers}.

(a) Which of the following are true:

(i) {triangle numbers} $\subset$ {counting numbers};
(ii) {multiples of 6} $\subset$ {multiples of 3};
(iii) {factors of 6} $\subset$ {factors of 18};
(iv) {multiples of 6} $\subset$ {multiples of 18}?

(b) Make a list of all the subsets of {a, e, i, o, u} which have four members.

In a class of 30 pupils, 23 study geography and 19 study history. Everyone studies either geography or history or both.
G represents {pupils who study geography}.
H represents {pupils who study history}.
The shaded region in Figure 1 represents G union H, which we write as G ∪ H.
G ∪ H has 30 members and we write n(G ∪ H) = 30.

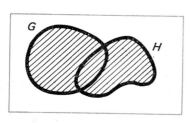

Fig. 1

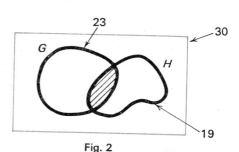

Fig. 2

The shaded region in Figure 2 represents G intersection H, which we write as $G \cap H$.
Find $n(G \cap H)$.

(c) Copy the diagram in Figure 3 and shade the region which represents $A \cup (B \cap C)$.

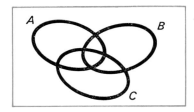

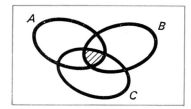

Fig. 3   Fig. 4

(d) What set does the shaded region in Figure 4 represent?

(e) If $n(P \cup Q) = 25$, $n(P) = 14$ and $n(Q) = 16$, draw a diagram to show this information, and find $n(P \cap Q)$.

(f) All the members of a club play either tennis or bowls or both. If the club has 40 members, 19 of whom play tennis and 7 of whom play both games, how many members play bowls?

7. OPERATIONS

Commutativity

An operation $*$ is commutative if
$$a * b = b * a$$
no matter what values we choose for a and b.

Figure 1 shows that $G \cup H = H \cup G$. Union is a commutative operation.

$3 - 2 = 1$. What is the value of $2 - 3$? Is subtraction commutative?

Associativity

An operation $*$ is associative if
$$(a * b) * c = a * (b * c)$$
no matter what values we choose for a, b and c.

$(12 \div 6) \div 2 = 2 \div 2 = 1$, but $12 \div (6 \div 2) = 12 \div 3 = 4$. Division is not associative.

Look carefully at Figure 4. Is $(A \cap B) \cap C$ the same as $A \cap (B \cap C)$?
Is $\cap$ associative?

(a) $a * b$ means 'multiply a by 2 and add b to the result'. For example, $3 * 1 = 6 + 1 = 7$.

Work out (i) $1 * 3$; (ii) $(3 * 1) * 2$; (iii) $3 * (1 * 2)$. What do your answers tell you about the operation $*$?

(b) If $\mathbf{A} = \begin{pmatrix} 2 & 1 \\ 0 & 6 \end{pmatrix}$, $\mathbf{B} = \begin{pmatrix} 3 & 4 \\ 1 & 1 \end{pmatrix}$ and $\mathbf{C} = \begin{pmatrix} 3 & 0 \\ 5 & 2 \end{pmatrix}$, work out $(\mathbf{AB})\mathbf{C}$ and $\mathbf{A}(\mathbf{BC})$. What do your answers suggest might be true about matrix multiplication?

8. PERCENTAGES

53% means $\frac{53}{100}$. 53% of £6 $= £\frac{53}{100} \times 6 = £3 \cdot 18$.

We can write a fraction as a percentage by first finding an equivalent fraction with bottom number 100. For example:

$$\tfrac{7}{25} = \tfrac{28}{100} = 28\%,$$

and

$$\frac{5}{9} = \frac{5 \times \frac{100}{9}}{9 \times \frac{100}{9}} = \frac{\frac{500}{9}}{100} = \frac{55\frac{5}{9}}{100} = 55\tfrac{5}{9}\%.$$

(a) Write these percentages as fractions in their simplest form:

(i) 80%;   (ii) $66\frac{2}{3}\%$;   (iii) 59%.

(b) Change these fractions to percentages:

(i) $\frac{47}{100}$;   (ii) $\frac{3}{8}$;   (iii) $\frac{5}{6}$.

(c) Work out:

(i) 15% of 60p;   (ii) 19% of 300;   (iii) $13\frac{1}{3}\%$ of £1500.

(d) Anne keeps £60 in her National Savings Bank account for one year· The interest rate is $3\frac{1}{2}\%$ each year. How much interest will she receive?

(e) A dealer bought a camera for £20 and sold it for £24.

(i) What profit did he make?

(ii) Express the profit as a fraction of the price the dealer paid.

(iii) Change the fraction to a percentage. This is called the percentage profit.

(f) Find the percentage profit on:

(i) a television set bought for £80 and sold for £110;

(ii) a bicycle bought for £30 and sold for £37·50.

(g) A man who earns £1850 per year is given a rise of 20%. What is his new salary?

9. Geometry

1. POLYGONS

The simplest shapes we have studied are *polygons*. Polygons have straight sides:

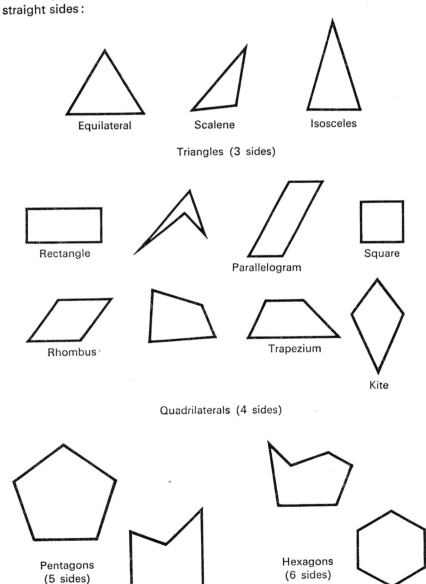

Equilateral   Scalene   Isosceles

Triangles (3 sides)

Rectangle   Parallelogram   Square

Rhombus ·   Trapezium   Kite

Quadrilaterals (4 sides)

Pentagons
(5 sides)

Hexagons
(6 sides)

1.1 Triangles

The inside angles of *any* triangle add up to 180°.

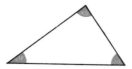

The marked angles add up to 180°.
This can be shown by the 'rotating pen' method:

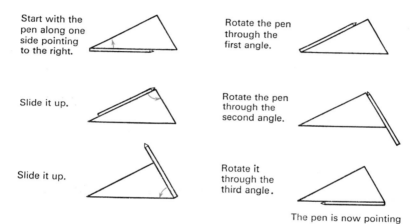

Start with the pen along one side pointing to the right.

Rotate the pen through the first angle.

Slide it up.

Rotate the pen through the second angle.

Slide it up.

Rotate it through the third angle.

The pen is now pointing to the left. It has turned through 180°.

1.2 Quadrilaterals

Any quadrilateral can be split into 2 triangles:

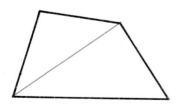

The angles of each triangle add up to 180°. Therefore the angles of a quadrilateral add up to twice 180°, that is 360°.

1.3 Pentagons

Any pentagon can be split up into 3 triangles:

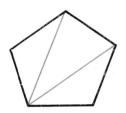
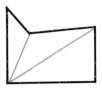

Use this method to find the sum of the angles of a pentagon.

1.4 Polygon check

1 Using the 'splitting into triangles' method, copy and complete this
  table:

Shape	Number of triangles	Sum of angles
Triangle	1	180°
Quadrilateral	2	360°
Pentagon	3	
Hexagon		
Heptagon (7 sides)		
Octagon		

2 Without using a protractor, work out the sizes of the lettered angles:

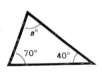
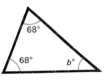
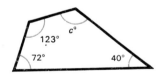

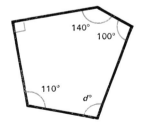
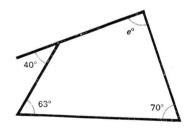

2. SYMMETRY

We have studied two types of symmetry for two-dimensional shapes:

Line symmetry

Rotational symmetry

This figure has rotational symmetry of order 6.

Line symmetry can be tested using a mirror.

Rotational symmetry can be tested using tracing paper.

2.1 Symmetry of polygons

A triangle with just one line of symmetry is called an *isosceles* triangle.

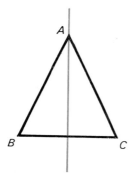

Because of the line of symmetry it follows that the sides *AB* and *AC* are equal in length, and the angles at *B* and *C* are equal.

A polygon is *regular* if it has rotational symmetry such that the order of rotational symmetry is equal to the number of sides. For example, a hexagon has 6 sides, and if its order of rotational symmetry is 6, it is regular.

A regular hexagon

Because of the rotational symmetry it follows that all the sides are equal in length, and all the angles are equal.

Since the angles of any hexagon add up to 720° (because it can be split into 4 triangles), each angle of a regular hexagon is 720° ÷ 6, that is 120°.

A regular three-sided polygon is called an *equilateral* triangle.

A regular four-sided polygon is called a *square*.

2.2 Symmetry check

1 What is the size of each angle of:
   (*a*) an equilateral triangle;
   (*b*) a square;
   (*c*) a regular pentagon;
   (*d*) a regular octagon?

2 One angle of an isosceles triangle is 40°. What are the sizes of the other angles? (There are two possible answers.)

3 Copy the next three figures. Mark in the lines of symmetry. Also mark the centres of rotational symmetry and state the order of rotational symmetry about each centre.

  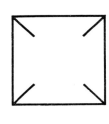

4 Draw diagrams of all the possible types of quadrilateral, and describe their symmetries.

5 Imagine a large *regular* pentagon marked out on the floor. If you walked round it, starting and finishing at *A*, you would have rotated through the five angles marked with arrows, and you would have made a complete turn. Use this information to work out the size of each of the marked angles.
   Hence work out the size of each of the inside angles of a regular pentagon. Check with your answer to Question 1 (*c*).

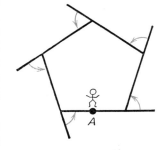

6 Repeat the method of Question 5 for a regular octagon.

7 A regular polygon has an angle of 140°. How many sides has it?

8 Can a regular polygon have an angle of 172°? If so, how many sides has it?

3.   POLYHEDRA

Some polygons will fit together to make solid shapes.

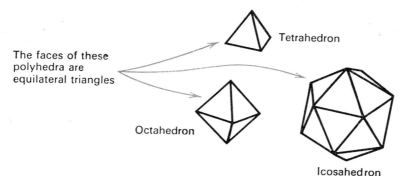

The faces of these
polyhedra are
equilateral triangles

Tetrahedron

Octahedron

Icosahedron

The faces of a cube
are squares:

The faces of a dodecahedron
are regular pentagons:

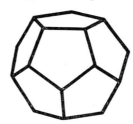

Polyhedra can be made by cutting out and folding up their *nets*.

This is a net for a cube:

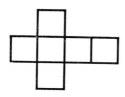

This is a net for an octahedron:

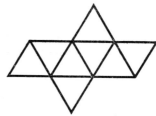

3.1   Symmetry in three dimensions

We have studied two types of symmetry:

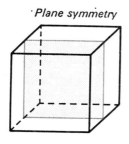

Plane symmetry

Rotational symmetry

Axis of
symmetry

The *symmetry number* of a solid shape is the number of ways in which it could be placed in a hole of the same shape.

For example, the symmetry number of this triangular prism is 6.

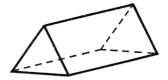

3.2 Polyhedra check

1 Copy and complete this table:

Polyhedra	Number of faces F	Number of vertices V	Number of edges E	F + V − E
Cube				
Tetrahedron				
Octahedron				
Icosahedron				
Dodecahedron				
Triangular prism				

You should find that the last column consists of 2's.

$F + V - E = 2$ is called *Euler's relation*.

2 A polyhedron has 5 faces and 8 edges. How many vertices must it have?

3 Draw four different nets for a cube.

4 Find how many different nets can be drawn for a tetrahedron.

5 Design a net for a square-based pyramid.

6 Two square-based pyramids are stuck together by their square faces. What polyhedron is formed?

7 How many planes of symmetry do these objects have?
  (*a*) A regular tetrahedron;
  (*b*) a square-based pyramid;
  (*c*) a cylinder;
  (*d*) a cube.

8 How many axes of symmetry do the objects in Question 7 have? What is the order of symmetry for each axis?

9 Find the symmetry numbers of the objects in Question 7.

4. TESSELLATIONS

Some polygons can be fitted together to make *tessellations* :

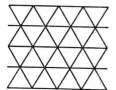 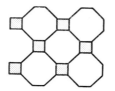 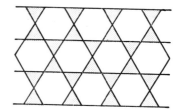

The sizes of the angles determine whether or not polygons will fit together without leaving gaps. For example :

Regular hexagons have angles of 120°, so three of them will fit together.

Regular pentagons have angles of 108°. Since three of these leave a gap, regular pentagons do not tessellate.

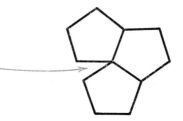

Some polygons which are not regular tessellate :

All triangles tessellate.

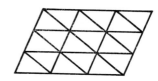

All quadrilaterals tessellate.

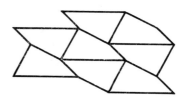

4.1   Solid tessellations

Some polyhedra fit together without leaving gaps:

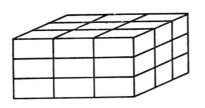
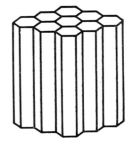

Cuboids   Hexagonal prisms

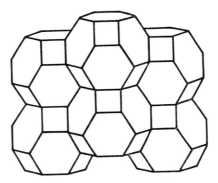

Truncated octahedra

4.2   Tessellation check

1   Make tessellations with each of the shapes in Figure 1.

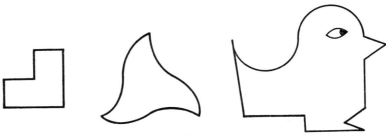

Fig. 1

2   Figure 2 is a net for a cubical box without
a lid. Make a tessellation with this net.
   Draw two more different nets for a cubical
box without a lid, and try to make tessellations
with the nets.

Fig. 2

3 Which of these polyhedra make solid tessellations?
   (*a*) Cubes;   (*b*) tetrahedra;
   (*c*) triangular prisms;   (*d*) octahedra;
   (*e*) prisms whose cross-sections are parallelograms.

5. TRANSFORMATIONS

In this section we shall look at the ways in which one shape can be *transformed* into another.

5.1 Reflections, rotations, translations

The work on symmetry led to two transformations:

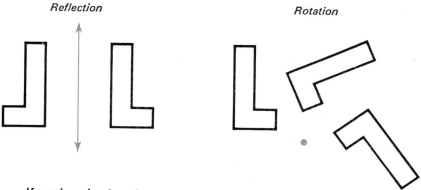

Reflection

Rotation

If a mirror is placed on the red line, the L's are reflections of each other.

The L's can be mapped onto each other by rotations about the red dot.

Another transformation which, like reflections and rotations, does not change the shape or size of the object is a *translation*.

This is just a slide without any rotation.

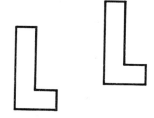

5.2 Reflection, rotation, translation check

1 Mark two points *A* and *B* on a piece of tracing paper (see Figure 3). By folding your paper find all the possible centres of rotation which would map *A* onto *B*.

85

A •

     • B

Fig. 3   Fig. 4

2 Trace the two F's in Figure 4. Fold to find the possible centres of rotation such that two corresponding points, the bottoms of the uprights, say, would rotate onto each other.

Repeat for another pair of corresponding points.

Where is the centre of rotation such that the **F**'s will rotate onto each other?

3 After a reflection or a rotation the image is the same shape and size as the object. How does the result of a reflection differ from the result of a rotation?

4 (*a*) What are the coordinates of the reflection of the point (2, 3) in the line $y = x$?

(*b*) The point (2, 3) is rotated through $90°$ anticlockwise about (0, 0). What are the new coordinates?

5 (*a*) The vector for a translation is $\binom{4}{5}$, that is, 4 'steps' to the right, and 5 'steps' up. What are the coordinates of the point obtained when this translation is applied to the point (2, 3)?

(*b*) What are the coordinates of the point which is mapped onto (5, 2) by this translation?

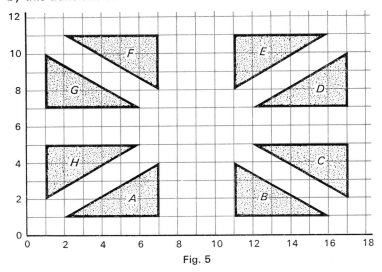

Fig. 5

6   In Figure 5, describe in full detail the transformations which would map:

(*a*) *A* onto *B*;   (*b*) *C* onto *D*;   (*c*) *D* onto *H*;

(*d*) *F* onto *A*;   (*e*) *G* onto *B*;   (*f*) *H* onto *E*.

5.3 Enlargements

Figure 6 shows another transformation, called an *enlargement*. The sides of the larger triangle are 3 times those of the smaller one. The *scale factor* is 3. *Note: OB* is 3 times *OA*.

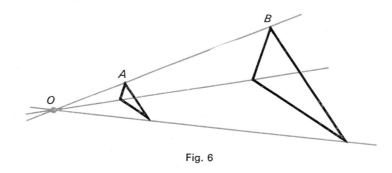

Fig. 6

Figure 7 shows a negative enlargement: the scale factor is -2.

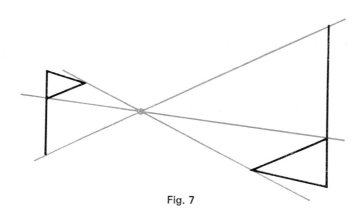

Fig. 7

Reflections, rotations and translations do not change shape or size. Enlargements do not change shape but they do change size. When objects have the same shape they are called *similar*.

5.4   Enlargement check

1   Copy the triangles in Figure 8 and enlarge them with scale factor 2
using the red dots as centres of enlargement.

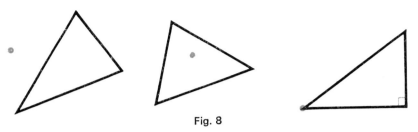

Fig. 8

2   Copy the diagrams in Figure 9 and enlarge the shapes with scale
factor $\frac{1}{2}$.

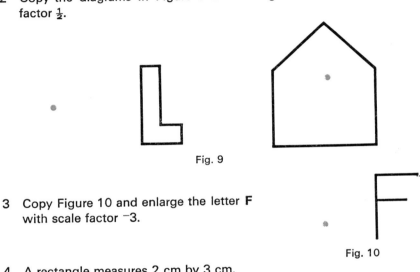

Fig. 9

3   Copy Figure 10 and enlarge the letter **F**
with scale factor ⁻3.

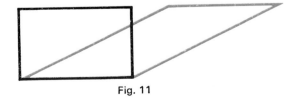

Fig. 10

4   A rectangle measures 2 cm by 3 cm.
(*a*) If it is enlarged with a scale factor of $1\frac{1}{2}$, what are the dimensions
of the enlarged rectangle?
(*b*) If the enlarged rectangle measures 14 cm by 21 cm, what is the
scale factor of the enlargement?
(*c*) Another rectangle measures 10 cm by 16 cm. Is it similar to the
rectangle measuring 2 cm by 3 cm? Explain your answer.

5.5   Shears

Figure 11 shows a
shear. The black
rectangle has been
sheared into the
red parallelogram.

Fig. 11

Note: (a) The area of the parallelogram is the same as the area of the rectangle (base × height).

(b) One line stays fixed; it is called the invariant line.

(c) All other points move parallel to the invariant line.

5.6 Shear check

1 Draw diagrams showing four possible shears of the red rectangle in Figure 12 with *AB* as the invariant line.

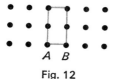

Fig. 12

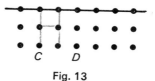

Fig. 13

2 Shear the **H** in Figure 13 so that *C* maps onto *D* using the black line as the invariant line.

5.7 Topology

The next diagram shows a transformation called a *topological transformation:*

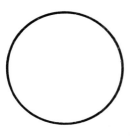

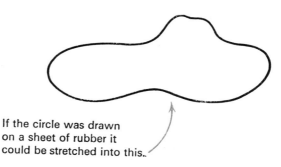

If the circle was drawn on a sheet of rubber it could be stretched into this.

The circle could also be stretched into the following shapes:

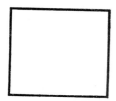

Topological transformations change shape and size. They are much more drastic than the other transformations we have dealt with.

In a topological transformation straight lines can become 'wiggly', but there will always be the same number of nodes, arcs and regions. For example, the network on the left can be transformed into any other network with 5 nodes, 8 arcs, and 5 regions (counting the outside) provided the order and relative positions of the nodes remain unchanged.

A polyhedron can be transformed into a network of lines. For example,

a cube 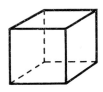 becomes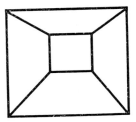

Imagine the front
face removed. Stretch
the front four vertices
backwards.

This is called a
Schlegel diagram.

5.8 Topology check

1 Draw some diagrams of your own showing topological transformations of a circle.

2 Draw a Schlegel diagram of a tetrahedron.

3 Copy and complete this table for the networks in Figure 14:

	Number of nodes	Number of regions	Number of lines
(a)			
(b)			
(c)			
(d)			

There is a connection between the numbers in the table. You have met a similar connection before. Explain.

(a)   (b)   (c)   (d)

Fig. 14

10. Measurement

1. LENGTH

When we measure length, we compare it with a fixed unit, for example, 1 metre (m).

Other common units of length are the kilometre (km), the centimetre (cm) and the millimetre (mm).

$$1 \text{ km} = 1000 \text{ m,}$$

$$1 \text{ cm} = \tfrac{1}{100} \text{ m,}$$

$$1 \text{ mm} = \tfrac{1}{1000} \text{ m.}$$

If we wish to find the number of words on this page, we can *count* the number of words and obtain an *exact* answer. If we wish to find the length of this page, we need to *measure* the length and *we cannot do this exactly.*

Since measurements are not exact, we need a way of stating how accurate they are. The length of this page is

23 cm to the nearest cm

or   23·3 cm to the nearest $\tfrac{1}{10}$ cm.

When we give a measurement to the nearest $\tfrac{1}{10}$ unit, we say that we give it to 1 decimal place.

If a rectangle is measured as 5·7 cm long and 4·3 cm wide to 1 decimal place, then

its true length lies between 5·65 cm and 5·75 cm, and
its true width lies between 4·25 cm and 4·35 cm.

What is the smallest perimeter that this rectangle could have? What is the largest perimeter?

Circumference of circle = π × diameter, where π = 3·1416 to 4 decimal places. Remember that the value you take for π will always be an approximation.

Copy and complete the following example and so find the length of the arc of a 120° sector cut from a circle of radius 10 cm (see Figure 1).

120° is $\frac{120}{360}$ of a complete turn.

Length of arc is therefore $\frac{}{360}$ of complete circumference

$$= \frac{120}{360} \times \pi \times 20 \text{ cm}$$

$$= \qquad \text{cm.}$$

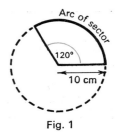

Fig. 1

(*a*) Find the circumference of a circle of diameter 12 cm. Take the value of π as 3·14.

(*b*) Find the length of the arc of a 72° sector cut from a circle of radius 17·5 cm. Take the value of π as $\frac{22}{7}$.

2. ROUNDING OFF

7·24 is nearer 7·2 than 7·3. We say that 7·24 = 7·2 to 1 decimal place.
7·26 is nearer 7·3 than 7·2. We say that 7·26 = 7·3 to 1 decimal place.
7·25 is halfway between 7·2 and 7·3, but it is customary to say that 7·25 is 7·3 to 1 decimal place.

We can also round off to a number of significant figures. For example:

8167 = 8000 to 1 S.F.	0·05378 = 0·05 to 1 S.F.
8167 = 8200 to 2 S.F.	0·05378 = 0·054 to 2 S.F.
8167 = 8170 to 3 S.F.	0·05378 = 0·0538 to 3 S.F.

(*a*) Write the following numbers to the nearest whole number:

  (i) 15·42;   (ii) 0·86;   (iii) 59·72.

(*b*) Write the following numbers to 2 decimal places:

  (i) 14·237;   (ii) 5·785;   (iii) 3·297.

(*c*) Write the following lengths to 3 S.F.:

  (i) 12·641 m;   (ii) 6238 cm;   (iii) 0·0048195 m.

3. AREA

Which of the shapes in Figure 2 has the larger area?

Fig. 2

We could measure area in triangles but, in fact, we choose a square as our basic unit. One common unit of area is the square centimetre (cm²):

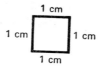

We estimate the area of an irregular figure by covering it with a transparent square grid and counting the squares.

Estimate in cm² the area of the shape in Figure 3.

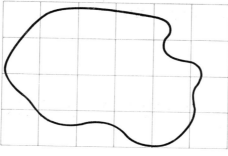

Fig. 3

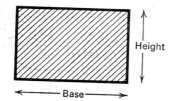

Area of rectangle = base × height.

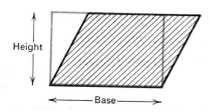

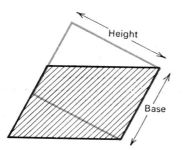

A parallelogram can be sheared into a rectangle of equal area. Therefore area of parallelogram

= base × height.

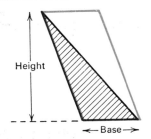

The triangle is half of the red parallelogram. Therefore area of triangle

$$= \tfrac{1}{2} \times \text{base} \times \text{height}.$$

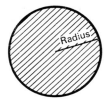

Area of circle $= \pi \times (\text{radius})^2$.

Copy and complete the following example and so find the area of a sector of angle 120° cut from a circle of radius 10 cm (see Figure 4).

Area of sector is $\frac{}{360}$ of area of whole circle

$$= \tfrac{120}{360} \times \pi \times 10^2 \ \text{cm}^2$$

$$= \quad \text{cm}^2.$$

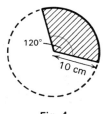

Fig. 4

Area of curved surface of cylinder $=$ circumference $\times$ height

$$= \pi \times \text{diameter} \times \text{height}.$$

Give an expression for the *total* surface area of a cylinder.

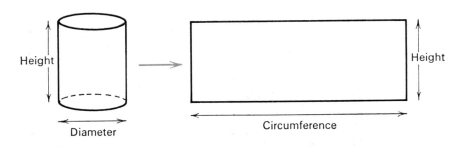

(*a*) Find the area of each of the shapes in Figure 5.

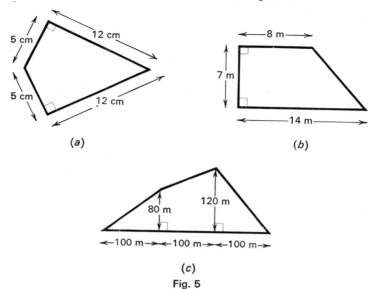

Fig. 5

(*b*) A rectangular block of wood is 10 cm long, 5 cm wide and 3 cm thick. Find its total surface area.

(*c*) Find the area of a circle of radius 35 cm. (Take the value of π as $\frac{22}{7}$.)

(*d*) Find the area of a sector of angle 60° cut from a circle of diameter 12 cm. (Take the value of π as 3·14.)

(*e*) Find the total surface area of a cylinder of radius 5 cm and height 15 cm. (Take the value of π as 3·14.)

4. RIGHT-ANGLED TRIANGLES

This diagram should remind you of Pythagoras's rule.

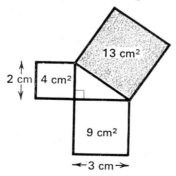

The rule states that the area of the square drawn on the longest side of *any* right-angled triangle is equal to the combined area of the squares on the other two sides.

The length of each side of the red square is $\sqrt{13}$ cm. Use any method to calculate this length correct to 3 S.F.

The longest side of a right-angled triangle is called the *hypotenuse*. If the length of the hypotenuse is r and the lengths of the other two sides are p and q, then $r^2 = p^2 + q^2$.

(a) Find r if $p = 8$ cm and $q = 6$ cm.

(b) Find q if $r = 5$ cm and $p = 4$ cm.

(c) Find p if $r = 13$ cm and $q = 5$ cm.

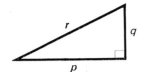

5. VOLUME

When we measure volume, we choose a cube as our basic unit. One common unit of volume is the cubic centimetre (cm^3) :

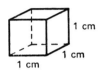

Volume of any prism $=$ area of base $\times$ height.

Volume of cuboid $=$ area of base $\times$ height

                 $=$ length $\times$ width $\times$ height.

Volume of cylinder $=$ area of base $\times$ height

                 $= \pi \times (\text{radius})^2 \times$ height.

Find the volume of each of the solids shown in Figure 6.

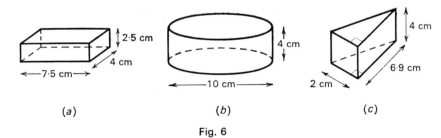

(a)   (b)   (c)

Fig. 6

6. RATIO

If air contains four times as much nitrogen as oxygen, we say that the ratio of nitrogen to oxygen is 4 to 1 and the ratio of oxygen to nitrogen is 1 to 4.

When we use a ratio to compare two quantities we must write both quantities in the same units. For example, the ratio of £2 to 75p is,

working in pence, 200 to 75 $=$ 8 to 3;

or, working in pounds, 2 to $\frac{3}{4}$ $=$ 8 to 3.

If £6000 is divided between three partners in the ratio of 2 to 3 to 5, there are $2+3+5 = 10$ shares.

The first partner gets $\frac{2}{10}$ of £6000

$$= £\tfrac{2}{10} \times 6000$$

$$= £1200.$$

How much each do the other two receive?

(*a*) Write the following ratios in their simplest form:

   (i) 15 to 20;   (ii) 250 to 100;   (iii) $\frac{1}{5}$ to 2;

   (iv) 4 to $2\frac{1}{2}$;   (v) £3 to 50p;   (vi) 40 m to 1 km.

(*b*) In a school of 855 pupils, there are 405 girls. What is the ratio of boys to girls?

(*c*) Copper sulphate is made from:

                    32 parts of copper,
                    16 parts of sulphur,
                    32 parts of oxygen,
                    45 parts of water.

Find the weight of copper, sulphur, oxygen and water in 7·5 kg of copper sulphate.

7. SIMILAR OBJECTS

When two objects have the same shape:

   (i) All the lengths of one object are a fixed number times the corresponding lengths of the other. This number is called the scale factor.

   (ii) Corresponding angles are equal.

Objects which have the same shape are called similar.

If the ratio of corresponding lengths of two similar objects is *a* to *b*, then the ratio of corresponding areas is a^2 to b^2, and the ratio of corresponding volumes is a^3 to b^3.

(*a*) The lengths of the shadows of a post and a tree are in the ratio of 5 to 9. If the height of the post is 4 m, what is the height of the tree?

(*b*) 1 kg of grass seed is needed for a rectangular plot 20 m long. How much seed would be needed for a similar plot 70 m long?

(*c*) Two similar cylinders have heights of 10 cm and 15 cm. Write down (i) the ratio of their diameters; (ii) the ratio of the areas of their bases; (iii) the ratio of their volumes.

If the area of the base of the larger cylinder is 27 cm², what is the area of the base of the smaller one?

11. Coordinates and graphs

1. NAMING POINTS

Write down the coordinates of each of the points in Figure 1. Start like this:
A (2, 3), B (,), ...

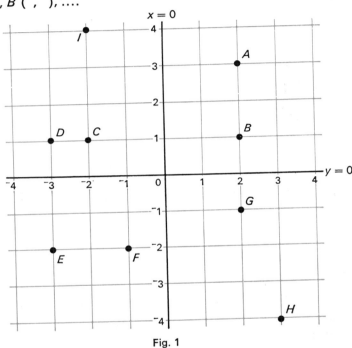

Fig. 1

2. SINES AND COSINES

(a) The x-coordinate of P is cos 32° and the y-coordinate of P is sin 32°.
Using your tables, copy and complete this statement:
P is the point with coordinates (,).

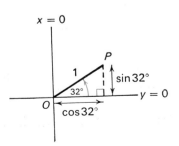

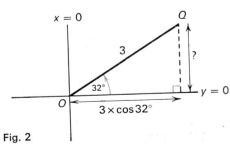

Fig. 2

(*b*) Copy and complete these statements:
The *x*-coordinate of *Q* is $3 \times \cos 32° = $.
The *y*-coordinate of *Q* is $3 \times$ $=$.
Q is the point with coordinates (,).

(*c*) Find the coordinates of points *R*, *S* and *T* in Figure 3. Notice that some of the coordinates, including the *x*-coordinate of point *R*, are negative.

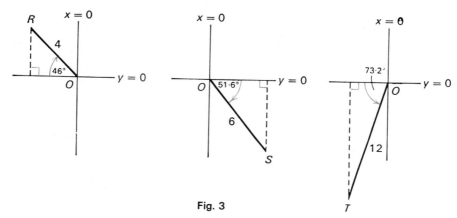

Fig. 3

3. LINES PARALLEL TO THE AXES

(*a*) What do you notice about the *x*-coordinates of the points *A*, *B* and *G* in Figure 1?
These points are all on the line with equation $x = 2$.
(*b*) Give the equations of the lines through:
    (i) *I* and *C*;   (ii) *D*, *C* and *B*;   (iii) *D* and *E*.
(*c*) On a coordinate diagram like Figure 1 show the lines $x = 1$, $x = {}^-4$, $y = 2$ and $y = {}^-3$. Label each of the lines with its equation.

4. REGIONS

The unshaded region in Figure 4 is $x > 2$.

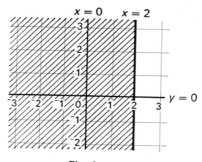

Fig. 4

Show each of the following regions on a separate diagram. In each case, leave unshaded the region you require.

(*a*) $x > 1$;   (*b*) $x < 2$;   (*c*) $x > {}^-2$;

(*d*) $y < 2$;   (*e*) $y < {}^-1$;   (*f*) $y > {}^-4$.

5. OTHER LINEAR GRAPHS

If you were asked to draw the graph of $y = 2x + 1$, you would have to find the coordinates of some points which fitted the equation, plot the points and join them up.

(*a*) What is the smallest number of points you would need?

(*b*) Why is it sensible to plot more points than this?

(*c*) Some points on the line $y = 2x + 1$ are (0, 1), (2,), ($^-2$,) and (, 7). Copy and complete these coordinates.

(*d*) Draw the graph of $y = 2x + 1$. Check that it is correct by looking at Figure 5.

(*e*) Now draw the graphs of:

(i) $y = 3x - 1$;   (ii) $x + y = 8$;   (iii) $x - y = 2$;

(iv) $x + 2y = 6$;   (v) $2y = x + 3$.

6. OTHER REGIONS

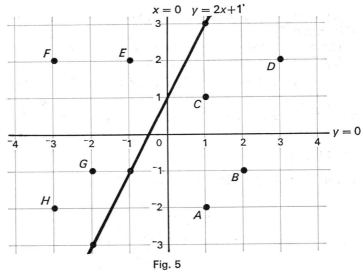

Fig. 5

Write down the coordinates of the points *A*, *B*, *C* and *D*. Do these points fit the relation $y > 2x + 1$ or $y < 2x + 1$?

Write down the coordinates of the points *E*, *F*, *G* and *H*. Do these points fit the relation $y > 2x + 1$ or $y < 2x + 1$?

Copy Figure 5, shade out the region $y < 2x + 1$ and so leave the region $y > 2x + 1$ unshaded.

Notice that the line divides the diagram into three parts:
all the points in the shaded region fit the relation $y < 2x+1$;
all the points on the line fit the relation $y = 2x+1$;
all the points in the unshaded region fit the relation $y > 2x+1$.
Show each of the following regions on a separate diagram and in each
case shade out the region you do *not* want.

(a) $y < 3x-2$;

(b) $y < 2(x-3)$;

(c) $y > \frac{1}{2}(x+5)$;

(d) $x+y < 9$.

7. GRADIENTS OF GRAPHS AND TANGENTS OF ANGLES

7.1 Gradients

Write down the gradient of each of the lines you drew in Section 5. You
may be able to do this just by looking at the equations. If not, measure the
gradients of your lines.

7.2 Tangents

Do you remember the connection between the gradient of a graph and the
tangent of the angle it makes with the $y = 0$ axis?

Use your tangent tables to work out the lengths and angles marked with
letters in Figure 6.

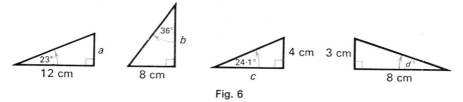

Fig. 6

8. WHERE GRAPHS CROSS

Figure 7 shows that (2, 6) is the
point where the graphs $y = 3x$ and
$x+y = 8$ cross. This means that the
values $x = 2$ and $y = 6$ fit both of
the equations $y = 3x$ and $x+y = 8$.

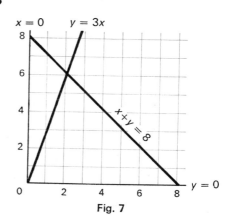

Fig. 7

101

For each of the following, draw the graphs and find the values of x and y which fit both of the equations. Do each question on a separate diagram and use axes as in Figure 7.

(a) $y = 2x$ and $x + y = 9$;   (b) $y = x + 1$ and $x + y = 7$;

(c) $y = 2x + 1$ and $y = x + 4$;   (d) $y = 2x + 1$ and $y = 5$.

Look again at the graph you drew for part (c). The x-coordinate of the point of intersection of the lines $y = 2x + 1$ and $y = x + 4$ is 3. $x = 3$ is the solution of the equation $2x + 1 = x + 4$.

Draw on one diagram the graphs of $y = 2(x - 1)$ and $y = 3x - 4$. From the point of intersection, give the solution of the equation

$$2(x - 1) = 3x - 4.$$

9. NON-LINEAR GRAPHS

Copy and complete this table for the graph of $y = \frac{1}{2}x^2$.

x	$^-3$	$^-2$	$^-1$	0	1	2	3
y	4·5			0	0·5		

Copy Figure 8, plot the other points and join them in a smooth curve to give the graph of $y = \frac{1}{2}x^2$.

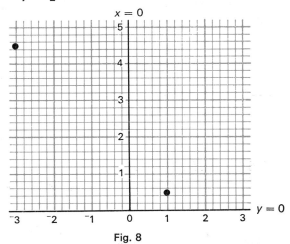

Fig. 8

(a) What is the equation of the line of symmetry of the curve $y = \frac{1}{2}x^2$?

(b) You could use your graph to solve the equation $\frac{1}{2}x^2 = 3$.
Draw the line $y = 3$ on the same diagram as the graph of $y = \frac{1}{2}x^2$. It will cut the curve in two points. The x-coordinates of these points are the solutions of the equation $\frac{1}{2}x^2 = 3$. What are these solutions ?

(c) Draw up a table of values for $y = 2x^2$ for $^-2 \leqslant x \leqslant 2$ (that is, for values of x from $^-2$ to 2). Mark out axes, choosing sensible scales.

Remember that you do not have to use the same scale on both axes. Draw the graph of $y = 2x^2$ for $^-2 \leqslant x \leqslant 2$ and use it to solve the equation $2x^2 = 5$.

(*d*) Draw the graph of $y = (x+1)^2$ for $^-4 \leqslant x \leqslant 3$. Remember to work out a table of values before marking out the axes. Use your graph to solve the equation $(x+1)^2 = 6$.

(*e*) Draw the graph of $y = (\frac{1}{2}x)^2$ for $^-4 \leqslant x \leqslant 4$ and use it to solve the equation $(\frac{1}{2}x)^2 = 2\cdot5$.

10. GRAPHS WITH PRACTICAL APPLICATIONS

(*a*) Some graphs have practical applications. For example, Figure 9 shows how the cost of hiring two cars, *A* and *B*, depends on the distance travelled.

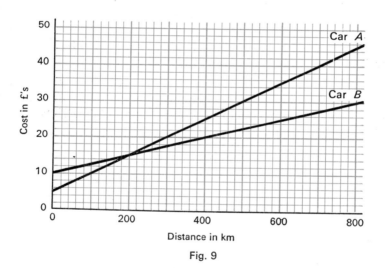

Fig. 9

The cost of hire consists of a basic charge and a charge per kilometre. The basic charge for car *A* is £5. What is the basic charge for car *B*?
Which car would work out cheaper for a 500 km journey?
What meaning can you give to the point where the two lines cross?
Work out the cost per kilometre, excluding the basic charge, for each car.

(*b*) On Tuesday, William set out on an afternoon walk. He started at 2 p.m., walked for an hour at exactly 5 km per hour, rested for half an hour, and then walked for another hour at 5 km per hour, by which time he had reached a friend's house where he stayed. Draw a graph to show William's journey to his friend's house.

(*c*) Figure 10 shows a journey Cyril made on Wednesday. Describe this journey as fully as possible.

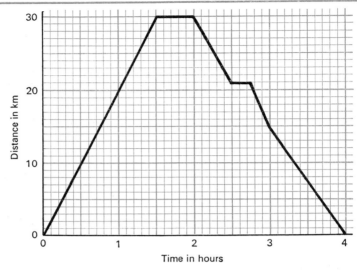

Fig. 10

Do you think he was walking? If not, how do you think he was travelling? His name might give you a clue.

(*d*) Figure 11 is a graph for currency conversion. It enables you to change from Korean money (wan) to English money (pence), or of course vice versa. Copy the graph but extend it to 100p. How many wan will you need to go up to?

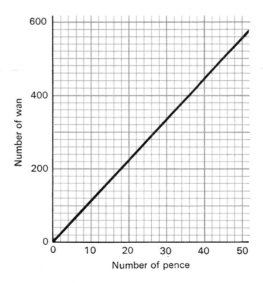

Fig. 11

Use your graph to answer these questions:

(i) How many wan are equivalent to 25p?

(ii) How many pence are equivalent to 840 wan? (Give your answer to the nearest penny.)

12. Statistics

Some of the chapters included in this series form part of a fairly new study called *statistics*. As its name implies, statistics grew from the State wanting to know more about its people, its commerce and industry. As populations grew and the economic and social life of a country became more complicated, the older methods of government, and particularly of raising taxes, were not sufficient. More accurate and detailed information was needed to assess the present and to predict the future, and this vast amount of information had to be sorted and classified.

Nowadays, statistics has much wider applications. Students and people in a great many jobs — engineers, doctors, scientists, linguists, economists and farmers, to mention just a few, make use of the subject to help them in their work and research.

Let us take as an example a school which is investigating the possibility of having its own swimming pool. It is found that a suitable pool is going to cost £2000 and the education authority will provide half the cost if the school can raise the other £1000. There follow some of the aspects of this project:

A questionnaire distributed to people living in the area

'Do you think that Fivefield school should have its own swimming pool?'

Yes	
No	
Don't care	

Take the result of this opinion poll as, Yes – 924, No – 112, Don't care – 224, and present this as a bar chart and as a pie chart.

If 1800 forms were distributed, what percentage was returned?

The cost of pools

(a) If there are 800 pupils in the school, what is the mean average cost per head?

(b) The graph in Figure 1 shows the cost of a pool, such as the one the school has in mind, over the past six years.

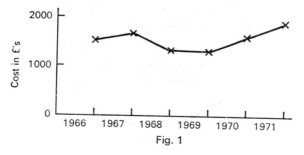

Fig. 1

Why are the points on the graph joined by straight lines? What do you think the cost of the pool might be next year? Should the school wait in the hope that prices will come down?

Reaching the target

(*a*) Draw a large 'thermometer' on which the running total of money collected could be recorded.

(*b*) What extra information does a graph like the one in Figure 2 give you?

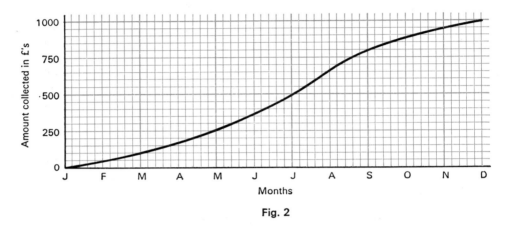

Fig. 2

By which month was half the money collected?
Can this type of graph ever slope downwards?

How the money was collected

(*a*) What fraction of the total was collected by each activity (see Figure 3)?

Fig. 3

(*b*) What is wrong with the bar chart in Figure 4?

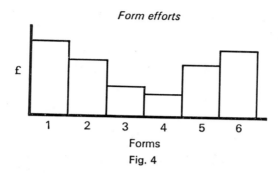

Form efforts

Forms

Fig. 4

1. DISPLAYING INFORMATION

The swimming pool project incorporated much of the work you have already met. Our study of statistics started with collecting and displaying information, and we saw we could use:

1.1 Tables

These are quite satisfactory when there are not many items, as on p. 105. The results could have been illustrated simply by:

Yes	924
No	112
Don't care	224

and left at that.

1.2 Bar charts

Figure 5 shows three different ways of drawing a bar chart.

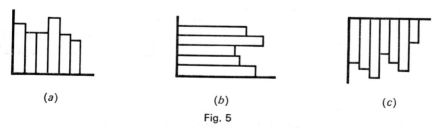

(*a*)   (*b*)   (*c*)

Fig. 5

Can you think of a survey where Figure 5 (*c*) might be appropriate?

Points to note with a bar chart are:
(*a*) The bars should not really touch, but it is often more convenient to draw them this way.
(*b*) Always label both axes fully and give the chart a title.

1.3 Pie charts

Why are they always circular? Could we have a rectangular pie chart (see Figure 6)?

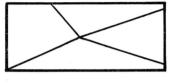

Fig. 6

A pie chart gives us a good idea at a glance of what fraction of the whole each part is. They are not so easy to draw as bar charts. Why?

1.4 Pictograms

These are really bar charts in disguise (see Figure 7).

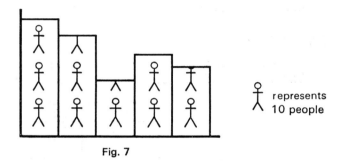

Fig. 7

Remember that graphs and charts can be misleading because 'Things are not always what they seem'.

2. REPRESENTATIVE VALUES

A representative value must be typical of all the values and is often called an *average*. There are three main types of average – 'The Three M's' – Mode, Mean and Median.

2.1 The mode

This is the most frequently occurring item.

2.2 The mean

This is the sum of all the values divided by the total number of values. Did you find that the mean cost per head for the swimming pool was £2000 ÷ 800 = £2·50?

2.3 The median

This is the middle value, once the values have been arranged in order of size.

(*a*) Find the mode, mean and median of the following numbers:

3, 5, 7, 6, 8, 7, 1, 3, 5, 7, 2.

(*b*) How would you find the median value of 1, 4, 7, 10?

(*c*) Can a collection of values have more than one mode, more than one median, more than one mean? If your answer to any of these is 'yes', try to illustrate it with an example.

When we want to find the mean of a group of values which are all close to each other, we can save some work by the following short cut. For example, to find the mean of 151, 152, 150, 149, 151, 150, write the numbers as:

$(150+1)$, $(150+2)$, $(150+0)$, $(150-1)$, $(150+1)$, $(150+0)$.

The mean is then
$$150 + \frac{1+2+0-1+1+0}{6}$$
$$= 150 + \tfrac{3}{6}$$
$$= 150\tfrac{1}{2}.$$

(*d*) Find the mean of 243, 239, 240, 244, 238, 241, 239, 240.

3. FREQUENCY TABLES

Sometimes you will want to find the mean from a frequency table. In terms of the swimming pool project, the following collection (in pence) might have been made at the door for a House Play:

2, 10, 10, 2, 50, 2, 5, 10, 5, 10, 10, 5, 50, 10, 10, 2, 1, 5, 5, 5, 5, 2,
2, 50, 1, 10, 10, 5, 5, 10, 50, 2, 50, 5, 10, 10, 5, 10, 10, 2, 10, 10,
10, 1, 50, 2, 2, 10, 10, 10, 2, 10, 5, 10.

Collect together these results and complete a copy of the following table:

Value of coin in p	Frequency	Value × Frequency
1	3	
2	11	
5	12	
10	22	
50	6	
Total		

How can you find the mean from this table? Carry out the necessary division and check that the mean is $11\tfrac{11}{54}$p.

Do you think that this is the best sort of average to use here? Is there any other representative value which might seem more appropriate?

Statistics

Can you think of a way, other than a table, in which these results can be represented?

Project

Using the percentage marks from a recent examination or test for your own class:
(*a*) Calculate the true mean mark.
(*b*) *Estimate* the mean mark by using a completed copy of the following table:

Marks	Half-way mark m	Frequency f	$m \times f$
0–20			
21–40			
41–60			
61–80			
81–100			
Total			

How close is the estimated value to the true value?

4. CUMULATIVE FREQUENCY

It is possible that parents and senior pupils might have helped with some of the work in the construction of the pool such as digging and landscaping the surround. The following grouped frequency table shows how long they might have spent.

Time spent in hours	Number of people (frequency)
0–5	2
6–10	3
11–15	4
16–20	6
21–25	9
26–30	7
31–35	3
36–40	1

Complete a cumulative frequency column and hence draw a cumulative frequency graph. How many people worked on the pool altogether? What was the median number of hours worked?
Use the cumulative frequency graph to find the upper and lower quartiles. What is the inter-quartile range?

13. Probability

Figure 1 shows a fixed disc and a rotating arrow. The circular disc has only red and white sectors which are all the same size. If the arrow is spun freely, what is the probability that it will not stop on the same colour four times running in four spins?

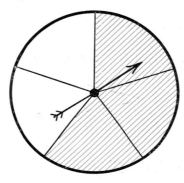

Fig. 1

Before we try to answer this question, let us see what happens with a smaller number of spins.

(a) One spin

If the arrow is spun freely, what is the probability that it will stop on a red sector? Is there more than one way of trying to solve this problem?

We could spin the arrow a large number of times and record the success fraction. If we spin it 1000 times and succeed in obtaining 'red' 609 times, what is our success fraction? Does this give an estimate of the required probability?

Are stopping on red and stopping on white equally likely events? The sectors are all the same size. Is the arrow equally likely to stop on any one of the five sectors? How many of them are red? Write down the probability that the arrow will stop (i) on a red sector, (ii) on a white sector. What is the ratio of the probability of stopping on red to the probability of stopping on white?

See if you can design a disc which has only red and white sectors such
that the probabilities of stopping on red and white sectors are in the ratio
1 to 2. Use a circle of radius 5 cm to represent the disc and make an
accurate drawing to show a possible arrangement of the sectors. State
your sector angles clearly and mark each sector 'red' or 'white'. Is there
more than one possible arrangement of the sectors?

(*b*) *Two spins*

The tree diagram in Figure 2 shows the possible outcomes for two
consecutive spins. Copy and complete this diagram by writing the
appropriate probability on each branch of the tree.

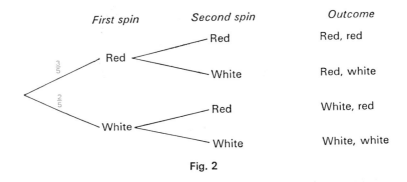

Fig. 2

Use your tree diagram to help you to complete a copy of the following
table:

Outcome	Probability
Red, red	$\frac{3}{5} \times \frac{3}{5} = \frac{9}{25}$
Red, white	$\frac{3}{5} \times \frac{2}{5} = \frac{6}{25}$
White, red	
White, white	

What is the probability that the arrow will

(i) stop on the same colour twice running;

(ii) not stop on the same colour twice running?

What is the sum of these two probabilities? Give an explanation for
your answer.

(*c*) *Three spins*

Draw a tree diagram to show the possible outcomes for three consecutive spins.

Use your diagram to help you to find the probability that the arrow will
  (i) stop on the same colour three times running;
 (ii) not stop on the same colour three times running.

Explain how you could have found the answers to these questions if,
instead of drawing the whole tree diagram, you had drawn only the
branches shown in Figure 3.

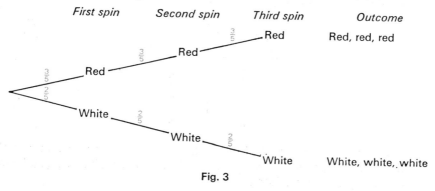

Fig. 3

(d) *Four or more spins*

Now try to answer the question at the beginning of the chapter, that is,
find the probability that the arrow will not stop on the same colour four
times running in four spins.

Write down an expression for the probability that the arrow will not
stop on the same colour five times running in five spins.

The rules of a game which can be played with the spinner state:
for stopping on red – score 3 and await your next turn;
for stopping on white – score 2 and spin again unless you have had
four spins already.

List the scores which it is possible to obtain with just one turn.

Copy and complete the tree diagram in Figure 4 and hence find the
probability of obtaining each of these scores.

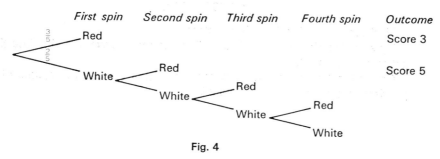

Fig. 4

(e) *Simulation with a spinner*

The table below gives the results of a traffic survey: the number of commercial vehicles (for example, lorries, vans, buses) in 40 sets of 10 vehicles travelling on a road were counted. There were 8 sets of 10 vehicles with 0 commercial vehicles in them, 9 sets of 10 vehicles with 1 commercial vehicle in them, etc.

Number of commercial vehicles	Frequency
0	8
1	9
2	14
3	7
4	2
5	0

We can make a model of this situation by designing a spinner so that the probability that the arrow stops at 0 is $\frac{8}{40}$, the probability that it stops at 1 is $\frac{9}{40}$, and so on (see Figure 5).

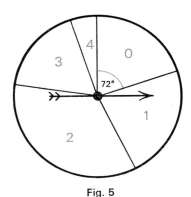

Fig. 5

The angle for the sector marked '0' is

$$\tfrac{8}{40} \times 360° = 72°.$$

Find the angles for the other sectors.

By spinning the arrow and recording the results, we can simulate the actual traffic count.

Count the traffic on a road near your school (or use the results of a previous count) and then simulate it.

14. Calculation

1. INDICES

$3^2 \times 3^4 = (3 \times 3) \times (3 \times 3 \times 3 \times 3) = 3 \times 3 \times 3 \times 3 \times 3 \times 3 = 3^6$.
Therefore $3^2 \times 3^4 = 3^{2+4} = 3^6$.

$$5^7 \div 5^3 = \frac{5 \times 5 \times 5 \times 5 \times 5 \times 5 \times 5}{5 \times 5 \times 5} = 5 \times 5 \times 5 \times 5 = 5^4.$$

Therefore $5^7 \div 5^3 = 5^{7-3} = 5^4$.

The scales on your slide rule make use of this idea. Numbers are marked on the rule so that, for example, the length of rule corresponding to 2 added to the length corresponding to 3 gives the length corresponding to 6:

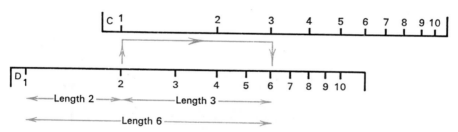

Length 2 + length 3 = length 6

$$2 \quad \times \quad 3 \quad = \quad 6$$

(a) Calculate, leaving your answer in powers of 10:

    (i) $10^2 \times 10^4$;   (ii) $10^7 \div 10^2$;   (iii) $10^0 \times 10^4$;

    (iv) $10^5 \div 10^4$;   (v) $10^2 \times 10^3 \times 10^4$.

(b) Use the mapping

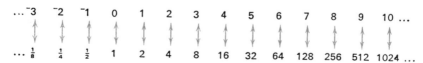

to work out:

    (i) 16×64;   (ii) $512 \div 32$;   (iii) $256 \times \frac{1}{8}$;

    (iv) $32 \div 256$;   (v) $\frac{1}{8} \times 512 \times \frac{1}{4}$;   (vi) $2 \times 128 \times \frac{1}{2}$.

2. SLIDE RULE

(a) Multiplication with two or more numbers

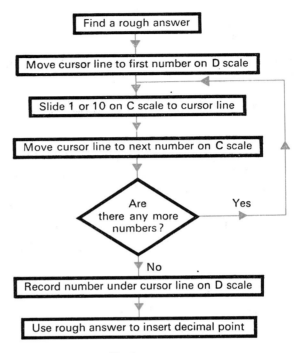

Fig. 1

Use your slide rule to find, as accurately as you can, the values of :

(i) $2 \cdot 4 \times 2 \cdot 9$;   (ii) $11 \cdot 6 \times 6 \cdot 7$;   (iii) $4 \cdot 7 \times 29$;

(iv) $15 \cdot 6 \times 14 \cdot 2$;   (v) $194 \times 7 \cdot 3$;   (vi) $3 \cdot 2 \times 2 \cdot 2 \times 1 \cdot 26$;

(vii) $83 \times 72 \times 5 \cdot 5$;   (viii) $0 \cdot 63 \times 2 \cdot 8 \times 540$; (ix) $0 \cdot 08 \times 0 \cdot 37 \times 17 \cdot 2$.

(*b*) *Division of one number by another*

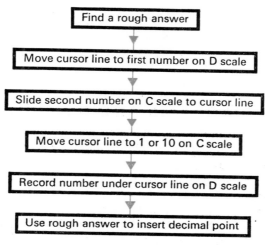

Fig. 2

Use your slide rule to find, as accurately as you can, the values of:

(i) $18 \cdot 6 \div 3 \cdot 5$;   (ii) $4 \cdot 8 \div 8 \cdot 6$;   (iii) $0 \cdot 054 \div 12 \cdot 2$.

(*c*) *Expressions such as* $\dfrac{5 \cdot 4 \times 3 \cdot 6}{6 \cdot 5}$

This is best done in the order $(5 \cdot 4 \div 6 \cdot 5) \times 3 \cdot 6$, as shown in Figure 3, because only one setting of the rule is then needed.

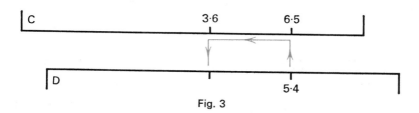

Fig. 3

Always try to arrange your calculations to use as few settings as possible.

Use your slide rule to perform the following calculations as accurately as you can. You will sometimes need to 'change ends'.

(i) $\dfrac{5 \cdot 4 \times 3 \cdot 6}{6 \cdot 5}$;   (ii) $\dfrac{118 \times 0 \cdot 6}{77}$;   (iii) $\dfrac{16 \cdot 4 \times 8 \cdot 2}{7 \cdot 5}$;

(iv) $\dfrac{65 \times 28}{32}$;   (v) $\dfrac{5 \cdot 8 \times 0 \cdot 43}{6 \cdot 9}$;   (vi) $\dfrac{3 \cdot 8 \times 9 \cdot 6}{12 \cdot 2}$.

117

(*d*) *Squares and square roots*

Use the *A* and *D* scales of your slide rule to work out:

(i) $(3 \cdot 6)^2$;   (ii) $(5 \cdot 5)^2$;   (iii) 65^2;   (iv) 320^2;

(v) $\sqrt{13}$;   (vi) $\sqrt{68}$;   (vii) $\sqrt{160}$;   (viii) $\sqrt{(0 \cdot 42)}$.

3. FLOW DIAGRAMS AND COMPUTERS

Computers can perform complicated calculations very quickly, but the calculations have first to be split up into easy steps. The first stage is to draw a flow diagram.

A flow diagram is a method of giving a set of instructions in a logical manner. It is particularly useful when some of them have to be repeated. See, for example, the flow diagram in Figure 1.

Questions which are placed in a diamond shaped box can only have 'yes' or 'no' answers because computers work on a 'yes' or 'no' system.

The connections between the basic units of a computer are shown in Figure 4.

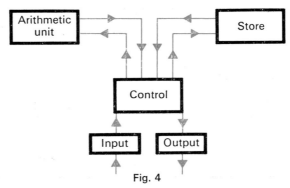

Fig. 4

(*a*) Write briefly about the function of each of the basic units shown in Figure 4.

(*b*) Write a program to compute the area, *A*, of the trapezium in Figure 5, where $A = \frac{1}{2}(a+b)h$. Start with inputs of *a*, *b* and *h* to stores *F*, *G* and *H*, respectively.

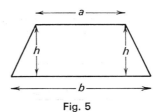

Fig. 5

118

(*c*) Work through the program in Figure 6. What sequence of numbers does it output from store *A* ?

A	B	C
0		
	3	
		10

(1) Input to *A*.
(2) Input to *B*.
(3) Input to *C*.
(4) Replace *A* by *A* + *B*.
(5) Replace *C* by *C* − 1.
(6) Output from *A*.
(7) If *C* > 0, go back to instruction (4).
(8) Finish.

Fig. 6

(*d*) Write a program which will output the first ten powers of 2, that is, 2, 4, 8, 16, ..., 1024.

4. STANDARD FORM

A very large number such as

$$369\,000\,000\,000\,000\,000$$

can be written more conveniently as $3 \cdot 69 \times 10^{17}$. This is called the *standard form* of the number.

Very small numbers can also be written more conveniently in this form. For example, in standard form

$$0 \cdot 000\,000\,000\,000\,068$$

would be $6 \cdot 8 \times 10^{-14}$.

To write a number in standard form, move the digits across the decimal point until the number lies between 1 and 10, then count the number of places, *n* say, that you have moved the digits *to the right* and multiply by 10^n.

Here are some more examples:

$$15\,600\,000\,000 = 1 \cdot 56 \times 10^{10},$$
$$63\,000\,000 \quad = 6 \cdot 3 \times 10^7,$$
$$0 \cdot 000\,0725 \quad = 7 \cdot 25 \times 10^{-5},$$
$$0 \cdot 001\,81 \quad = 1 \cdot 81 \times 10^{-3}.$$

(*a*) Write the following numbers in standard form:

(i) 1720;
(ii) 54 000 000;
(iii) 0·000 86;
(iv) 0·059.

(*b*) Write the following numbers in standard form to 2 S.F. :

(i) 64 715;
(ii) 144 359 000;
(iii) 0·000 087 52;
(iv) 0·006 183.

119

15. Matrices

1. STORING INFORMATION

Matrices can be used to store information. For example, we have used them to:

(*a*) store the results of football matches:

$$
\begin{array}{c}
& P \quad W \quad D \quad L \\
\begin{array}{c} \text{Liverpool} \\ \text{Everton} \\ \text{Leeds} \end{array}
\begin{pmatrix} 18 & 11 & 4 & 3 \\ 18 & 10 & 6 & 2 \\ 17 & \boxed{10} & 5 & 2 \end{pmatrix}
\end{array}
$$

Leeds won 10 matches.

(*b*) describe networks:

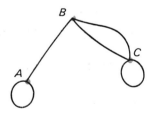

$$
\begin{array}{c}
& A \quad B \quad C \\
\begin{array}{c} A \\ B \\ C \end{array}
\begin{pmatrix} & & \\ & & \\ 0 & 2 & 2 \end{pmatrix}
\end{array}
$$

There are 2 direct routes
from *C* to *B*.

(*c*) describe relations:

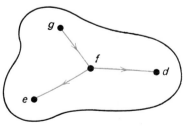

'is a parent of'

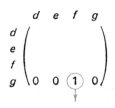

$$
\begin{array}{c}
& d \quad e \quad f \quad g \\
\begin{array}{c} d \\ e \\ f \\ g \end{array}
\begin{pmatrix} & & & \\ & & & \\ & & & \\ 0 & 0 & 1 & 0 \end{pmatrix}
\end{array}
$$

g is a parent of *f*.

120

(*d*) describe journeys:

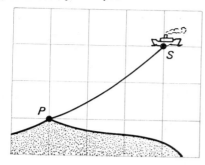

Scale: 1 cm represents 1 km.

$$\begin{pmatrix} 2 \end{pmatrix} \downarrow$$

The ship is 2 km north
of the port.

(*e*) describe shapes by stacking together journeys from the origin:

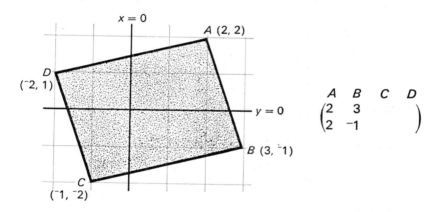

$$\begin{matrix} A & B & C & D \\ \begin{pmatrix} 2 & 3 & & \\ 2 & -1 & & \end{pmatrix} \end{matrix}$$

Copy and complete the matrices in (*b*), (*c*), (*d*) and (*e*).

The *order* of the matrix in (*a*) is 3 by 4. It has 3 *rows* and 4 *columns*. Remember that we always write the *row number first*.

Write down the order of the matrices in (*b*), (*c*), (*d*) and (*e*). Which of them are square matrices?

2. COMBINING MATRICES

We often label matrices with capital letters in heavy type like this:

$$\mathbf{A} = \begin{pmatrix} 5 & -2 \\ -1 & 2 \\ 4 & 3 \end{pmatrix} \quad \text{and} \quad \mathbf{B} = \begin{pmatrix} 2 & 0 \\ -5 & 1 \\ 3 & -1 \end{pmatrix}.$$

121

(*a*) We *add* matrices by adding the pairs of numbers which have corresponding positions in the matrices:

$$\mathbf{A} + \mathbf{B} = \begin{pmatrix} 5+\ 2 & {}^-2+\ 0 \\ {}^-1+{}^-5 & 2+\ 1 \\ 4+\ 3 & 3+{}^-1 \end{pmatrix} = \begin{pmatrix} 7 & {}^-2 \\ {}^-6 & \\ & \end{pmatrix}.$$

Copy and complete this addition.

(*b*) We can also *subtract* matrices:

$$\mathbf{A} - \mathbf{B} = \begin{pmatrix} 5-\ 2 & {}^-2-\ 0 \\ {}^-1-{}^-5 & 2-\ 1 \\ 4-\ 3 & 3-{}^-1 \end{pmatrix} = \begin{pmatrix} 3 & {}^-2 \\ 4 & \\ & \end{pmatrix}.$$

Copy and complete this subtraction.

We can *add* or *subtract* two matrices only if they have the *same* order. Why? What can you say about the order of the answer?

Matrix addition is commutative. For example,

$$\begin{pmatrix} 5 & {}^-2 \\ {}^-1 & 2 \\ 4 & 3 \end{pmatrix} + \begin{pmatrix} 2 & 0 \\ {}^-5 & 1 \\ 3 & {}^-1 \end{pmatrix} = \begin{pmatrix} 2 & 0 \\ {}^-5 & 1 \\ 3 & {}^-1 \end{pmatrix} + \begin{pmatrix} 5 & {}^-2 \\ {}^-1 & 2 \\ 4 & 3 \end{pmatrix}.$$

Is it also associative?

(*c*) We can multiply a matrix by a number:

$$5\mathbf{A} = \begin{pmatrix} 5\times\ 5 & 5\times{}^-2 \\ 5\times{}^-1 & 5\times\ 2 \\ 5\times\ 4 & 5\times\ 3 \end{pmatrix} = \begin{pmatrix} 25 & {}^-10 \\ {}^-5 & 10 \\ 20 & 15 \end{pmatrix}.$$

Find 3**B**.

(*d*) When we multiply two matrices, we combine each row of the first matrix with each column of the second matrix. Let us see this happen for the matrices

$$\mathbf{C} = \begin{pmatrix} 3 & 0 & 4 \\ 2 & {}^-1 & 1 \end{pmatrix} \quad \text{and} \quad \mathbf{D} = \begin{pmatrix} 1 & {}^-1 \\ 3 & 1 \\ 2 & 5 \end{pmatrix}.$$

The first row of **C** combines with the columns of **D** to give

$$(3 \quad 0 \quad 4) \begin{pmatrix} 1 \\ 3 \\ 2 \end{pmatrix} = 3 + 0 + 8 = 11$$

and

$$(3 \quad 0 \quad 4) \begin{pmatrix} {}^-1 \\ 1 \\ 5 \end{pmatrix} = {}^-3 + 0 + 20 = 17.$$

The second row of **C** combines with the columns of **D** to give

$$(2 \quad ^-1 \quad 1) \begin{pmatrix} 1 \\ 3 \\ 2 \end{pmatrix} = 2 + {}^-3 + 2 = 1$$

and

$$(2 \quad ^-1 \quad 1) \begin{pmatrix} ^-1 \\ 1 \\ 5 \end{pmatrix} = {}^-2 + {}^-1 + 5 = 2.$$

Stacking the rows gives

$$\begin{pmatrix} 3 & 0 & 4 \\ 2 & ^-1 & 1 \end{pmatrix} \begin{pmatrix} 1 \\ 3 \\ 2 \end{pmatrix} = \begin{pmatrix} 11 \\ 1 \end{pmatrix} \quad \text{and} \quad \begin{pmatrix} 3 & 0 & 4 \\ 2 & ^-1 & 1 \end{pmatrix} \begin{pmatrix} ^-1 \\ 1 \\ 5 \end{pmatrix} = \begin{pmatrix} 17 \\ 2 \end{pmatrix},$$

and now stacking the columns, we have

$$\mathbf{CD} = \begin{pmatrix} 3 & 0 & 4 \\ 2 & ^-1 & 1 \end{pmatrix} \begin{pmatrix} 1 & ^-1 \\ 3 & 1 \\ 2 & 5 \end{pmatrix} = \begin{pmatrix} 11 & 17 \\ 1 & 2 \end{pmatrix}.$$

Work out **DC**. Is matrix multiplication commutative?
Is it associative?

We can work out **EF** only if the number of elements in each row of **E** is equal to the number of elements in each column of **F**. Remember the domino pattern ·

If

$$\mathbf{E} = \begin{pmatrix} 1 & 0 & 1 \\ 1 & 1 & 0 \end{pmatrix} \quad \text{and} \quad \mathbf{F} = \begin{pmatrix} 1 & 0 & 1 & 1 \\ 1 & 1 & 0 & 1 \\ 1 & 1 & 1 & 0 \end{pmatrix},$$

does **EF** have a meaning? Does **FE** have a meaning?

Exercise

1 Work out the following multiplications *if they have a meaning*

(a) $(3 \quad 2) \begin{pmatrix} ^-1 \\ 3 \end{pmatrix}$;

(b) $(2 \quad ^-3 \quad 1) \begin{pmatrix} 1 \\ 2 \\ ^-1 \end{pmatrix}$;

(c) $(3 \quad 0 \quad 5) \begin{pmatrix} 2 \\ 7 \end{pmatrix}$;

(d) $(2 \quad ^-3 \quad 7 \quad 0) \begin{pmatrix} ^-1 \\ 4 \\ 0 \\ 9 \end{pmatrix}$.

2 $\mathbf{A} = \begin{pmatrix} 1 & 2 \\ 3 & 4 \end{pmatrix}$ and $\mathbf{B} = \begin{pmatrix} 3 & 4 \\ 1 & 2 \end{pmatrix}$.

Find:

(a) $\mathbf{A} + \mathbf{B}$;   (b) $\mathbf{B} - \mathbf{A}$;   (c) $\mathbf{AB}$;   (d) $\mathbf{B}^2$.

3 Work out:

   (a) $\begin{pmatrix} 3 & 6 \\ -2 & 5 \end{pmatrix} \begin{pmatrix} -2 \\ 1 \end{pmatrix}$;

   (b) $(4 \quad -7) \begin{pmatrix} 1 & 0 \\ 0 & 1 \end{pmatrix}$.

4 $P = \begin{pmatrix} 1 & 5 \\ 2 & -3 \end{pmatrix}$, $Q = \begin{pmatrix} 2 & -4 \\ 1 & 0 \end{pmatrix}$ and $R = \begin{pmatrix} 4 & 0 & 3 \\ 1 & 1 & 0 \end{pmatrix}$.

   Find, where possible,

   (a) **PQ**;   (b) **PR**;   (c) **RQ**;   (d) **PQR**.

5 $A = \begin{pmatrix} 2 & 1 \\ 0 & -3 \\ 7 & 2 \end{pmatrix}$ and $B = \begin{pmatrix} 1 & -3 \\ -2 & 6 \\ 0 & 5 \end{pmatrix}$.

   Find:

   (a) **A − B**;   (b) **3A**;   (c) **5B**;   (d) **3A + 5B**.

6 $X = \begin{pmatrix} 1 & 0 & 2 \\ -3 & 2 & 0 \\ -1 & 1 & 3 \end{pmatrix}$, $Y = \begin{pmatrix} 2 & 0 \\ 0 & -1 \\ 3 & 2 \end{pmatrix}$ and $Z = \begin{pmatrix} -3 & -2 & 2 \\ -9 & 7 & 3 \\ 2 & 1 & 0 \end{pmatrix}$.

   Find, where possible,

   (a) **X + Y**;   (b) **X + Z**;   (c) **XZ**;   (d) **ZY**;   (e) **Y²**.

3. ROUTE MATRICES

A one-stage route matrix gives the number of direct routes between the nodes of a network.

   If a network has no one-way routes, then

   (i) its one-stage route matrix is symmetrical about the leading diagonal (top left to bottom right);

   (ii) the numbers on the leading diagonal are even.

   Multiplying a one-stage route matrix by itself gives the two-stage route matrix.

   Copy and complete the following examples.

Example 1

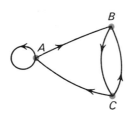

The one-stage route matrix is

$$R = \begin{pmatrix} 1 & 1 & 0 \\ 0 & 0 & 1 \\ 1 & 1 & 0 \end{pmatrix},$$

and the two-stage route matrix is

$$R^2 = \begin{pmatrix} 1 & 1 & 0 \\ 0 & 0 & 1 \\ 1 & 1 & 0 \end{pmatrix} \begin{pmatrix} 1 & 1 & 0 \\ 0 & 0 & 1 \\ 1 & 1 & 0 \end{pmatrix} = \begin{pmatrix} 1 & 1 & 1 \\ & 1 & \\ & & \end{pmatrix}.$$

Example 2

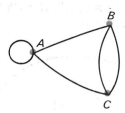

The one-stage route matrix is

$$S = \begin{pmatrix} 2 & 1 & 1 \\ 1 & & \\ 1 & & \end{pmatrix},$$

and the two-stage route matrix is

$$S^2 = \begin{pmatrix} 2 & 1 & 1 \\ 1 & & \\ 1 & & \end{pmatrix} \begin{pmatrix} 2 & 1 & 1 \\ 1 & & \\ 1 & & \end{pmatrix} = \begin{pmatrix} 6 & & \\ & & \\ & & \end{pmatrix}.$$

Find R^3 and S^3. What information do these matrices give?

(a) Write down matrices which describe the networks in Figure 1.

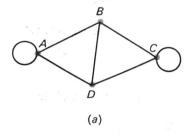

(a)   (b)

Fig. 1

(b) Draw the network described by the matrix

$$\begin{array}{c} \\ \text{From} \end{array} \begin{array}{c} \\ A \\ B \\ C \\ D \end{array} \overset{\displaystyle \text{To}}{\overset{\displaystyle A \; B \; C \; D}{\begin{pmatrix} 0 & 1 & 2 & 1 \\ 1 & 0 & 1 & 1 \\ 2 & 1 & 0 & 1 \\ 1 & 1 & 1 & 0 \end{pmatrix}}}.$$

(c) Write down the one-stage route matrix for the network in Figure 2.

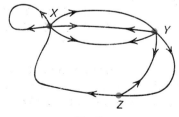

Fig. 2

Work out the two-stage route matrix.
How many two-stage routes are there from (i) X to Z; (ii) Y to X?

4. MATRICES AND RELATIONS

Figure 3 (*a*) shows the relation 'is on the left of' on a set of six dancers and Figure 3 (*b*) the relation 'is opposite to' on the same set.

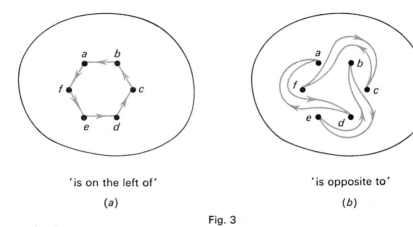

'is on the left of'

(*a*)

'is opposite to'

(*b*)

Fig. 3

The matrix which represents the relation 'is on the left of' is

$$
\mathbf{L} = \begin{pmatrix}
0 & 0 & 0 & 0 & 0 & 1 \\
1 & 0 & 0 & 0 & 0 & 0 \\
0 & 1 & 0 & 0 & 0 & 0 \\
0 & 0 & 1 & 0 & 0 & 0 \\
0 & 0 & 0 & 1 & 0 & 0 \\
0 & 0 & 0 & 0 & 1 & 0
\end{pmatrix}.
$$

A new matrix can be formed from **L** by interchanging the rows and columns, that is, the first row of **L** becomes the first column of the new matrix and so on. This new matrix is called the *transpose* of **L**.

$$
\text{The transpose of } \mathbf{L} = \begin{pmatrix}
0 & 1 & 0 & 0 & 0 & 0 \\
0 & 0 & 1 & 0 & 0 & 0 \\
0 & 0 & 0 & 1 & 0 & 0 \\
0 & 0 & 0 & 0 & 1 & 0 \\
0 & 0 & 0 & 0 & 0 & 1 \\
1 & 0 & 0 & 0 & 0 & 0
\end{pmatrix}
$$

and represents the relation 'has on the left' or 'is on the right of'. Draw a diagram to show this relation and check that your diagram looks like the one in Figure 3 (*a*) except that the arrows are reversed.

Write down the matrix which represents the relation 'is opposite to'. Call it **O**. Now write down the transpose of **O**. What relation does this represent? What happens when you reverse the directions of the arrows in Figure 3 (*b*)?

The diagram in Figure 3 (*a*) can be thought of as a network for which **L** is the one-stage route matrix. So

$$L^2 = \begin{pmatrix} 0 & 0 & 0 & 0 & 1 & 0 \\ 0 & 0 & 0 & 0 & 0 & 1 \\ 1 & 0 & 0 & 0 & 0 & 0 \\ 0 & 1 & 0 & 0 & 0 & 0 \\ 0 & 0 & 1 & 0 & 0 & 0 \\ 0 & 0 & 0 & 1 & 0 & 0 \end{pmatrix}$$

is the two-stage route matrix and represents the relation 'is on the left of the left of'. See Figure 4.

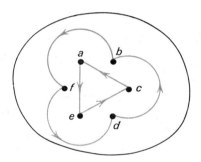

'is on the left of the left of'

Fig. 4

Work out O^2. Draw a diagram to show the relation which O^2 represents. What is this relation ?

$$LO = \begin{pmatrix} 0 & 0 & 0 & 0 & 0 & 1 \\ 1 & 0 & 0 & 0 & 0 & 0 \\ 0 & 1 & 0 & 0 & 0 & 0 \\ 0 & 0 & 1 & 0 & 0 & 0 \\ 0 & 0 & 0 & 1 & 0 & 0 \\ 0 & 0 & 0 & 0 & 1 & 0 \end{pmatrix} \begin{pmatrix} 0 & 0 & 0 & 1 & 0 & 0 \\ 0 & 0 & 0 & 0 & 1 & 0 \\ 0 & 0 & 0 & 0 & 0 & 1 \\ 1 & 0 & 0 & 0 & 0 & 0 \\ 0 & 1 & 0 & 0 & 0 & 0 \\ 0 & 0 & 1 & 0 & 0 & 0 \end{pmatrix}$$

$$= \begin{pmatrix} 0 & 0 & 1 & 0 & 0 & 0 \\ 0 & 0 & 0 & 1 & 0 & 0 \\ 0 & 0 & 0 & 0 & 1 & 0 \\ 0 & 0 & 0 & 0 & 0 & 1 \\ 1 & 0 & 0 & 0 & 0 & 0 \\ 0 & 1 & 0 & 0 & 0 & 0 \end{pmatrix}.$$

Figure 5 shows the relation which **LO** represents. Check that this relation is 'is on the left of the dancer opposite to'.

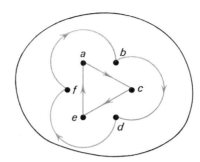

'is on the left of the dancer opposite to'

Fig. 5

What relation do you think **OL** represents?

(*a*) Copy and complete Figure 6 to show the relation 'is a prime factor of' on the set {2, 3, 4, 6, 8}.

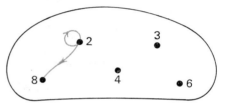

'is a prime factor of'

Fig. 6

Write down the matrix which represents this relation.

(*b*) Figure 7 shows the relation 'is a parent of' on the set {*a, b, c, d*}.

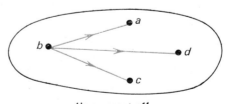

'is a parent of'

Fig. 7

(i)   Write down the matrix which describes this relation.
(ii) Draw a similar diagram to show the relation 'is a child of' on the same set.
(iii) Write down the matrix which describes the relation 'is a child of'.
(iv) What is the connection between the two matrices?

5. TRANSFORMATION MATRICES

Write down the 2 by 4 matrix which shows the journeys from the origin to the vertices of the unit square *OABC* (see Figure 8).

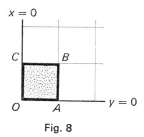

Fig. 8

Multiply this matrix by $\begin{pmatrix} 4 & 5 \\ 3 & 2 \end{pmatrix}$ on the left, that is, work out

$$\begin{matrix} & O & A & B & C \\ \begin{pmatrix} 4 & 5 \\ 3 & 2 \end{pmatrix} & \begin{pmatrix} 0 & 1 & 1 & 0 \\ 0 & 0 & 1 & 1 \end{pmatrix} \end{matrix} = \begin{matrix} O_1 & A_1 & B_1 & C_1 \\ \left(\right) \end{matrix}.$$

Draw a diagram to show the square *OABC* and its image $O_1A_1B_1C_1$ after the transformation represented by $\begin{pmatrix} 4 & 5 \\ 3 & 2 \end{pmatrix}$.

Calculate the area of the parallelogram $O_1A_1B_1C_1$.

What is the connection between the numbers in a transformation matrix and the effect it has on the area of a shape?

(*a*) Draw diagrams to show the effects on the unit square of the transformations whose matrices are:

(i) $\begin{pmatrix} 2 & 0 \\ 1 & 3 \end{pmatrix}$; (ii) $\begin{pmatrix} 1 & -1 \\ 1 & 1 \end{pmatrix}$; (iii) $\begin{pmatrix} 3 & 4 \\ 4 & -3 \end{pmatrix}$; (iv) $\begin{pmatrix} 1 & 2 \\ 3 & 6 \end{pmatrix}$.

In each case, find the area of the image of the unit square.

(*b*) Describe the transformation which each of the following matrices represents:

(i) $\begin{pmatrix} 0 & -1 \\ -1 & 0 \end{pmatrix}$; (ii) $\begin{pmatrix} 1 & 0 \\ 0 & -\frac{1}{2} \end{pmatrix}$; (iii) $\begin{pmatrix} -2 & 0 \\ 0 & -2 \end{pmatrix}$; (iv) $\begin{pmatrix} 1 & -3 \\ 0 & 1 \end{pmatrix}$.

6. TRANSFORMATIONS COMBINED

Draw a diagram to show the effect on the unit square of the shear represented by $\mathbf{S} = \begin{pmatrix} 1 & 2 \\ 0 & 1 \end{pmatrix}$. Label the image $O_1A_1B_1C_1$.

129

Now transform $O_1A_1B_1C_1$ by the rotation represented by

$$\mathbf{R} = \begin{pmatrix} 0 & -1 \\ 1 & 0 \end{pmatrix}.$$

Show the new image on your diagram and label it $O_2A_2B_2C_2$.

Compare your diagram with Figure 9 which shows the unit square and its image under *the shear represented by* **S** *followed by the rotation represented by* **R**.

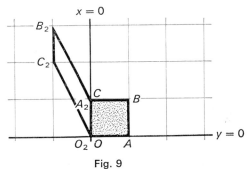

Fig. 9

The matrix for this combined transformation can be found by working out **RS** (not **SR** !).

Work out **RS** and check that $O_2A_2B_2C_2$ is the image of $OABC$ under the transformation represented by **RS**.

You may find it helpful to think of **S** as the matrix which 'gives the image under the shear of', **R** as the matrix which 'gives the image under the rotation of' and **RS** as the matrix which 'gives the image under the rotation of the image under the shear of'.

Draw a diagram to show the effect on the unit square of each of the following pairs of transformations and find the matrix which represents the equivalent single transformation:

(*a*) the one-way stretch represented by $\begin{pmatrix} 1 & 0 \\ 0 & 3 \end{pmatrix}$ followed by the shear represented by $\begin{pmatrix} 1 & -2 \\ 0 & 1 \end{pmatrix}$;

(*b*) the enlargement represented by $\begin{pmatrix} 5 & 0 \\ 0 & 5 \end{pmatrix}$ followed by the rotation represented by $\begin{pmatrix} \frac{3}{5} & -\frac{4}{5} \\ \frac{4}{5} & \frac{3}{5} \end{pmatrix}$;

(*c*) the transformation represented by $\begin{pmatrix} 1 & 0 \\ 2 & 3 \end{pmatrix}$ followed by the transformation represented by $\begin{pmatrix} 3 & -2 \\ 1 & 0 \end{pmatrix}$.

Revision exercises

ALGEBRA

1 For each of these questions, say whether the statement is true or false. If it is false, give the correct answer.

(a) $6 \times {}^{-}\frac{1}{2} = 3$;
(b) $3 \div {}^{-}1 = {}^{-}3$;
(c) ${}^{-}3 + 2 = {}^{-}1$;
(d) $3({}^{-}2 + 3) = 15$;
(e) ${}^{-}2(3 + {}^{-}2) = {}^{-}2$;
(f) ${}^{-}2 - {}^{-}5 = 3$.

2 Draw mapping diagrams for:

(a) $x \rightarrow x - 1$;
(b) $x \rightarrow x - 2$;
(c) $x \rightarrow x - 3$.

3 Draw mapping diagrams for:

(a) $x \rightarrow {}^{-}3x$;
(b) $x \rightarrow {}^{-}2x$;
(c) $x \rightarrow {}^{-}x$;
(d) $x \rightarrow {}^{-}\frac{1}{2}x$;
(e) $x \rightarrow {}^{-}\frac{1}{3}x$.

4 Use the mapping diagrams you drew in Question 3 to solve the equations:

(a) ${}^{-}2x = 6$;
(b) ${}^{-}\frac{1}{3}x = {}^{-}1$;
(c) ${}^{-}\frac{1}{2}x = 2$.

5 Solve each of these equations by the method of your choice:

(a) ${}^{-}2x + 3 = {}^{-}7$;
(b) $9 - 2x = {}^{-}1$;
(c) $6(7 - x) = 9$;
(d) $8 - \dfrac{2}{x} = 4$;
(e) $\frac{1}{2}(3x + 4) = 2$;
(f) $3(4 + 2x) = {}^{-}12$.

6 $y = \frac{1}{2}x^2$.

(a) What is y when x is 2?
(b) What is y when x is ${}^{-}2$?
(c) If y is 8, find two possible values for x.

7 Tangerines cost 2p each and grapefruit cost 5p each.

(a) What is the cost of t tangerines and g grapefruit?
(b) Liz has a maximum of 20p to spend on tangerines and grapefruit. Write this information as an algebraic expression.
(c) Show on a graph all the possible ways in which Liz can spend some or all of her money.

Revision exercises

8 (a) A boy is asked his age and says 'If you add 3 to my age and double the answer you will get 26'.

(i) Calling his age x, write this sentence as an equation.

(ii) How old is the boy?

(b) A second boy says 'You can find my age by solving the equation $2x - 25 = {}^-3$'.

(i) What is his age?

(ii) Explain, in words, his method of giving his age.

9 $s = \left(\dfrac{u+v}{2}\right) t.$

(a) Find s if $u = 0$, $v = 8$ and $t = 5$.

(b) Find s if $u = 7$, $v = {}^-2$ and $t = 4$.

(c) Find t if $s = 21$, $u = 4$ and $v = 2$.

10 (a) Draw mapping diagrams for $x \to x - 4$ and its inverse. Label the inverse mapping.

(b) Draw mapping diagrams for $x \to 4 - x$ and its inverse. Label the inverse mapping.

(c) Solve these equations. Explain your working: do not just write down the answers. Flow diagrams are acceptable.

(i) $4(x - 4) = 10$; (ii) $4(4 - x) = 10$;

(iii) $4 - 2x = 10$; (iv) $2x - 4 = 10$.

NUMBER

1 Express in prime factors: (a) 30; (b) 56; (c) 63; (d) 72. Write your answers in index form.

2 Write down the value of:

(a) 0.3×0.3; (b) $0.08 \div 0.002$.

3 If $Q = \{\text{quadrilaterals}\}$ and $R = \{\text{regular polygons}\}$, what is $Q \cap R$?

4 Say which of the following numbers are irrational:

(a) $\sqrt{64}$; (b) $\frac{22}{7}$; (c) $\sqrt{7}$; (d) π; (e) 3.14.

5 The operation $*$ means 'multiply the first number by the second and then divide by 2'. For example, $3 * 4 = \frac{12}{2} = 6$.
Work out (a) $10 * 7$; (b) $7 * 10$.
What do your answers tell you about the operation $*$?

6 Work out $\frac{4}{3} \div \frac{5}{9}$.

7 Find the exact value of $\dfrac{4000 \times 0.035}{0.05}$.

8 Multiply 1101_{two} by 101_{two}. Give your answer in base two.

9   Express $\frac{3}{5}$, $\frac{12}{25}$ and their product as exact decimals.

10 If $n(A \cup B) = 20$, $n(A \cap B) = 5$ and $n(B) = 14$, draw a diagram to illustrate this information and find $n(A)$.

11 The operation o is commutative. Copy and complete this operation table:

o	a	b	c	d
a	d	b	c	a
b		d	a	b
c			d	c
d				d

12 Find 6% of £11·30. Give your answer correct to the nearest penny.

13 Copy and complete the arrow diagram in Figure 1 to show the relation 'is a prime factor of' on the set {2, 5, 10, 20, 40}.

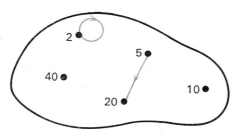

'is a prime factor of'

Fig. 1

14 Multiply 14_{six} by six, giving your answer in (a) base six; (b) base ten.

15 Find the exact value of

(a) $1·9 \times 0·304$;   (b) $1·9 \div 0·304$.

16 The 9600 shares in a company are owned by three men A, B and C. A owns $\frac{3}{8}$ of them and B owns 360 fewer than A. How many shares does C own?

17 In a class of 35 girls, all play either hockey or netball or both. 25 play hockey and 18 play netball.

(a) Draw a diagram to show this information.
(b) How many girls play hockey only?

18 A and B are subsets of the set $\mathscr{E} = \{1, 2, 3, 4, 5, 6\}$.
Give suitable examples of sets A and B such that

(a) $A \cup B = \mathscr{E}$;   (b) $A \subset B$;   (c) $n(A \cap B) = 0$.

19 Calculate the Compound Interest on £200 at 8% each year for 2 years.

20 State a fraction whose value lies between $\frac{2}{5}$ and $\frac{3}{7}$.

21 Give an example of:

(*a*) an integer;

(*b*) a rational number;

(*c*) an irrational number.

22 During a sale a shopkeeper reduced the price of an article from £4·50 to £3·96. What is the reduction as a percentage of the original price? Find the sale price of an article originally priced at £5·75 if this reduction was made in the same ratio as the first.

23 Make two copies of Figure 2. On one shade the region which represents $(P \cup Q) \cup R$ and on the other that which represents $P \cup (Q \cup R)$. What can you say about the operation $\cup$?

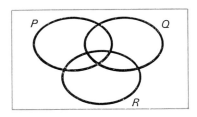

Fig. 2

24 If $p = 5·04$, $q = 4·6$, $r = 3·27$ and $s = 0·42$, calculate the exact value of:

(a) $p+q-r$;   (b) rs;   (c) $\dfrac{p}{s}$;   (d) $(p+r)(q-s)$.

25 Jane sorted her records into the following sets:

	Vocal (*V*)		Not vocal (*V'*)	
	Pop (*P*)	Not pop (*P'*)	Pop (*P*)	Not pop (*P'*)
Long playing (*L*)	6	5	3	4
Extended play (*E*)	0	3	1	*z*
Single (*S*)	10	*x*	5	*y*

Use the table to find:

(a) $n(L)$;   (b) $n(P' \cap V \cap E)$;

(c) $n(P \cap S)$;   (d) $n[L \cup (P \cap V)]$.

Jane had lent some of her records to friends and was unable to fill in the spaces marked *x*, *y* and *z* until she remembered that

$$n(V \cup P) = 35, \quad n(S \cup L) = 36 \quad \text{and} \quad n(P') = 19.$$

Using this extra information and the table, find the values of *x*, *y* and *z*.

26 An arithmetic is based on a clock-face which shows the figures 0, 1, 2, 3, 4.

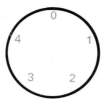

In this arithmetic a number is represented by its remainder when it is divided by 5. For example, 6 is written as 1, 9 is written as 4 and 12 is written as 2.

Copy and complete the following operation tables for the arithmetic.

+	0	1	2	3	4
0			2		
1					
2					1
3	3			1	
4					

×	0	1	2	3	4
0		0			
1					
2	0				
3				4	2
4					

(*a*) State the identity for addition in this arithmetic.

(*b*) State the inverse of 3 under multiplication.

(*c*) How can you tell from the tables whether the operations are commutative?

(*d*) Use the tables to help you to solve the equations

(i) $x+3 = 2$; (ii) $4x = 1$; (iii) $2x+4 = 0$.

GEOMETRY

1 Calculate the lettered angles in Figure 3.

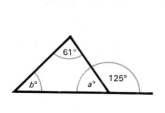
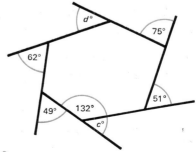

Fig. 3

2 (a) Use compasses to construct an equilateral triangle whose sides are of length 4 cm.

(b) By building more equilateral triangles on the one you have drawn in (a), construct a regular hexagon.

3 (a) Draw a circle of radius 4 cm. Using a protractor, mark 'spokes' at 72° intervals (see Figure 4). Join up the ends of the spokes to make a regular pentagon.

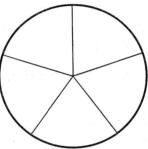

Fig. 4

(b) What would be the angle between the spokes for a regular octagon? Construct a regular octagon by the method described in (a).

(c) Use this method to draw a regular hexagon.

(d) Try to find a quicker method of drawing a regular hexagon in a circle without using a protractor. Try to explain why your method works.

4 Which of the following regular polygons tessellate? Calculate the angle gap for those that do not.

(a) Triangles;   (b) quadrilaterals;

(c) pentagons;   (d) hexagons;

(e) octagons.

5 Draw (if possible) diagrams with the following symmetry:

(a) one line of symmetry only, no rotational symmetry;

(b) no lines of symmetry, rotational symmetry of order 4;

(c) 3 lines of symmetry only, no rotational symmetry.

6 Figure 5 shows part of an infinite repeating pattern. Describe all the single transformations which would map the pattern onto itself.

Fig. 5

7 Copy this table and put a tick in the appropriate column if the given property is unchanged under the given transformation :

	Rotation	Reflection	Translation	Enlargement	Shear
Length					
Angle					
Shape					
Area					

8 Are all rectangles similar?
Are all squares similar?
Are all circles similar?
Explain your answers.

9 Draw Schlegel diagrams for a square-based pyramid:
(*a*) by removing the base,
(*b*) by removing a triangular face.

10 (*a*) Which of the networks in Figure 6 are traversable (that is, can be drawn without taking your pen off the paper or going over any line twice)?

(*a*)   (*b*)   (*c*)   (*d*)

Fig. 6

(*b*) In Figure 6 (*a*) there are 3 arcs meeting at *A*: *A* is an odd node. There are 4 arcs meeting at *B*: *B* is an even node.

How many odd nodes are there in Figure 6 (*a*)? How many even nodes?

Copy and complete this table for each network in Figure 6. Draw some more networks of your own and include them in the table.

	Number of odd nodes	Number of even nodes	Is network traversable?
(*a*)			
(*b*)			
(*c*)			
(*d*)			

What is the rule for finding whether or not a network is traversable?

MEASUREMENT

1 Write 4·277 to:

   (*a*) 1 decimal place;

   (*b*) 3 significant figures;

   (*c*) the nearest whole number.

2 The length of each side of a square is 5·2 cm to the nearest tenth of a centimetre. Find the smallest possible perimeter of the square.

3 Sketch the triangle whose vertices are at (3, 1), (6, 1) and (5, 3) and find its area.

4 Figure 7 shows a right-angled triangle and a semi-circle. Calculate the area of the semi-circle.

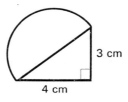

3 cm

4 cm

Fig. 7

5 1 litre of liquid weighs 1 kg. What does 1 cm³ of the liquid weigh? (1 litre = 1000 cm³.)

6 In a pie chart showing a family's weekly expenditure, the angle of the sector representing food is 112°. If the total expenditure was £27, how much was spent on food?

7 Figure 8 shows a cylindrical seat of radius 0·3 m and height 0·5 m.

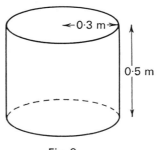

←0·3 m→

0·5 m

Fig. 8

(*a*) Taking π = 3, estimate the total surface area in square metres.

(*b*) You wish to make a cover for the seat. Give two reasons why you would have insufficient material if you bought the number of square metres which you have given as your answer to (*a*).

8   In a doll's house the height of each of the 15 steps in the stairs is 1·3 cm to the nearest tenth of a centimetre. What is the greatest possible height between the two floors? What is the least possible height?

9   On a map whose scale is 1 to 100 000 a lake is represented by a region of area 2·8 cm². What is the corresponding area on a map whose scale is 1 to 50 000?

10 Figure 9 shows a solid with uniform cross-section. All the angles are right-angles.

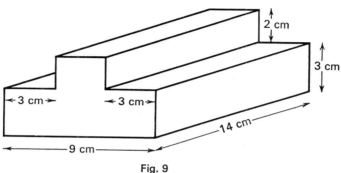

Fig. 9

(*a*) Calculate the area of the cross-section in cm².

(*b*) Calculate the volume of the solid, stating the units that you use.

11 A hollow pipe has an internal diameter of 6 cm and is 5 mm thick. Its length is 1 m. Calculate the volume of material which makes up the pipe.

12 The three sides of a triangle are 5·4 cm, 3·8 cm and 2·8 cm to the nearest 0·1 cm. What is the smallest perimeter the triangle could have?

13 A firm makes Christmas decorations by spraying circular discs, radius 3 cm, on both sides with gold paint.

(*a*) Calculate the area of one side of one disc. Take the value of π as 3·14.

(*b*) If 250 discs are to be sprayed on *both sides*, find the total area which has to be sprayed.

(*c*) The costing department estimates that spraying with gold paint costs 0·1p per cm². Find the cost of spraying 250 discs.

(*d*) The cost of cutting cardboard into discs of the required size is £1·96 per 1000 discs. Find the total cost to the manufacturer of fulfilling an order for 250 decorations.

14 *PQRS* is a quadrilateral in which the diagonal *PR* = 6·0 cm, angles *PRQ* and *RPS* are right-angles, *QR* = 1·2 cm, *PS* = 4·0 cm. Calculate the area of the quadrilateral.

15 Figure 10 represents a spool of recording tape. The shaded area with internal radius 3 cm and external radius 8 cm is occupied by tape. Calculate the shaded area.

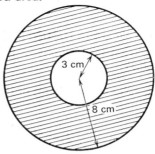

Fig. 10

16 If the circumference of a circle is doubled, what happens to:

(*a*) its diameter;   (*b*) its area?

17 A circular cone has a base of diameter 15·0 cm and a slant height of 18·0 cm. Calculate its vertical height.

18 A parallelogram of sides 12 cm and 6 cm has one pair of opposite sides 8 cm apart. What is the distance between the other pair of opposite sides?

19 In a scale model of a building, the ground area is $\frac{1}{100}$th of the actual ground area. What is the ratio of the volume of the building to the volume of the model?

20 Calculate the curved surface area of a cylinder with diameter 8·6 cm and height 12·4 cm.

21 A 400 m running track is to have two parallel straights of 80 m each and two semi-circular ends. What should be the radius of the semi-circles?

22 The boundary of the shaded figure consists of three semi-circular arcs, the smaller ones being equal (see Figure 11).

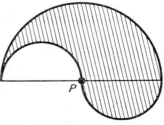

Fig. 11

(*a*) What is the ratio of the area of the whole of the larger semi-circle to that of one of the smaller semi-circles?

(*b*) What shape is formed by the shaded figure together with its image under a half-turn about *P*?

(*c*) If the area of one of the smaller semi-circles is *A* cm², find the area of the shaded figure in terms of *A*.

23 An object travelled with constant speed for 12 seconds, covering a distance of 60 m. Then its speed was uniformly retarded and the object came to rest 8 seconds later.

(*a*) Draw a graph to show the relation between speed and time during these 20 seconds.

(*b*) Calculate the total distance travelled in these 20 seconds.

24 The lower part of a jewel box is in the shape of a cuboid and the lid is in the shape of a pyramid. When the lid is closed, the vertex, *V*, of the pyramid is directly above the centre of the base of the cuboid. The external height of the pyramid is 5 cm and the external dimensions of the cuboid are 24 cm by 20 cm by 15 cm (see Figure 12).

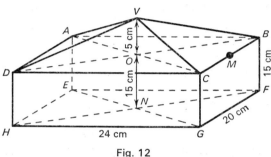

Fig. 12

(*a*) State the number of planes of symmetry of the jewel box.

(*b*) Find the external volume of the jewel box. State your units clearly. (The volume of a pyramid is $\frac{1}{3} \times$ base area × height.)

(*c*) *M* is the mid-point of the edge *BC*. *Calculate* the length of *VM*.

(*d*) Calculate the area of triangle *VBC*. State your units clearly.

(*e*) Calculate the *total* surface area of the outside of the jewel box.

COORDINATES AND GRAPHS

1 Mark two axes from ⁻6 to 6, and draw on the same diagram the graphs of $y = x$, $y = x+1$, $y = x+2$, $y = x+3$, $y = x+4$ and $y = x+5$. What do you notice about the lines?

Now draw the lines $y = x+6$ and $y = x-1$. Were these lines where you expected them to be?

2 Mark axes as in Question 1 and draw the graphs of $y = x-1$, $y = 2x-1$, $y = 3x-1$ and $y = 4x-1$. Through what point do all of these lines pass? Write down the equations of two other lines which also pass through this point.

3 Draw on one diagram the graphs of $y = \frac{1}{2}x^2$, $y = x^2$, $y = 2x^2$ and $y = 3x^2$. (Use values of x from $^-4$ to 4 and values of y from 0 to 16.) What do you notice about the graphs?

4 Mark axes as in Question 1. Draw the lines $y = 4$ and $x = ^-2$. Leave unshaded the region in which $y > 4$ and $x < ^-2$.

5 Mark axes as in Question 1 and draw the lines $y = 2x$ and $y = x+3$.
(a) What values of x and y fit both of the equations $y = 2x$ and $y = x+3$?
(b) What is the solution of $2x = x+3$?
(c) Leave unshaded the region where $y < x+3$ and $y > 2x$.

6 (a) By drawing two graphs on the same diagram, find two pairs of values which fit both of the equations $y = \frac{1}{2}x^2$ and $y = 2x$.
(b) Using one of the graphs you drew in part (a), find the two solutions of the equation $\frac{1}{2}x^2 = 5$.

7 Mark axes with values of x from $^-2$ to 5, and values of y from 0 to 14.
(a) Draw the following graphs: (i) $y = 2x+5$; (ii) $y = 8-x$.
(b) Mark with a small circle the point which gives the solution of the equation $2x+5 = 8-x$.
(c) Now draw the graph of $y = 3x^2$ on the same diagram.
(d) Find from your graphs the solutions of the equations:

   (i) $3x^2 = 2x+5$;   (ii) $8-x = 3x^2$.

8 The area of a circle is given by the approximate formula $A = 3r^2$.

(a) Draw up a table of values giving the areas of circles of radius 0·5 cm, 1 cm, 1·5 cm and 2 cm.
(b) Show these values on a graph.
(c) Use the graph to find approximate values of:

   (i) the area of a circle of radius 1·2 cm;
   (ii) the radius of a circle of area 10 cm².

9 Find the lengths and angles marked with letters in Figure 13.

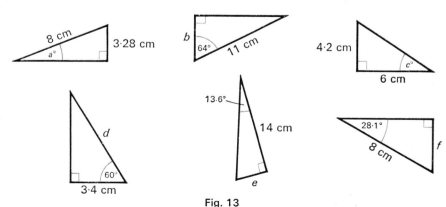

Fig. 13

10 A road slopes upwards at 8° to the horizontal. A man walks 200 m along the road.

(a) Draw a rough sketch to show this.

(b) Use trigonometry tables to calculate his increase in height.

11 A ladder leans against a wall so that the angle between the ladder and the wall is 24°. The ladder is 5 metres long. Use sine and cosine tables to calculate:

(a) the distance of the foot of the ladder from the wall;

(b) how far the ladder reaches up the wall.

12 The Havacar Company makes a basic charge of £3 per day for hiring a car. In addition they charge an extra 80p for each 100 km travelled.

(a) Copy and complete this table:

Distance travelled in km	0	50	100	150	200	250	300
Cost in pence	300		380				

(b) Draw a graph to show the cost of a day's hire for distances of up to 300 km.

(c) Use your graph to answer these questions as accurately as possible:

(i) What is the cost of the hire for a distance of 120 km?

(ii) What distance would have been covered if the charge was £4·50?

STATISTICS

1 Here is a list of subjects for statistical surveys. Plan the method and details of each survey, collect and display the results, and see if use can be made of an average value. Comment on the results and decide whether any conclusions are possible.

(a) The pets we keep.

(b) Left-handed, right-handed, boys and girls.

(c) Numbers of brothers and sisters.

(d) Number of times absent in a term.

(e) Best school meal of the week.

(f) Library issues.

(g) Most popular T.V. programme.

(h) What day of the week is your birthday?

(i) How long does it take you to get to school?

2 The first year in a mixed school is divided into four forms, 1 A, 1 B, 1 C and 1 D. Some of the pupils are in the 10 +, some in the 11 + and some in the 12 + age groups.

Design a table so that numbers can be placed in it to show form, age and sex as well as the totals in each category.

3 What sort of diagram would you choose to show the different shoe sizes worn by pupils in your class? Give reasons for your choice and carry out such a survey.

4 A recent survey showed that out of a group of 30 fifth-formers, 7 played the guitar, 13 played the piano, 4 played the violin and 6 did not play any instrument. None of those questioned played more than one instrument. Show this information on a pie chart, stating the sector angles clearly.

5 Here is a table showing the number and types of car observed during a survey:

Ford	BLMC	Vauxhall	Volkswagen	Others
45	55	43	27	10

Display this information by a pictogram.

6 (a) Find the mean of 2, 5, 7, 8, 9.
   (b) *Write down* the mean of 200, 500, 700, 800, 900.
   (c) *Write down* the mean of 232, 235, 237, 238, 239.

7 The marks of sixteen candidates in an examination were 61, 53, 40, 46, 52, 50, 36, 41, 71, 38, 47, 64, 54, 45, 32, 73. Find the mean and the median marks.
   Two more candidates took the examination later on and raised the mean mark by 0·25. Find the mean mark of these two candidates.

8 The mean of one group of six numbers is $8\frac{1}{2}$ and the mean of another group of eight numbers is $7\frac{1}{4}$. Find the mean of the combined group of fourteen numbers.

9 Calculate the median, mode and mean of the following groups of numbers:
   (a) 1, 1, 2, 2, 2, 2, 2, 3, 3, 4;
   (b) 1, 1, 2, 2, 3, 3, 3, 3, 3, 4;
   (c) ⁻1, ⁻1, ⁻2, ⁻2, ⁻2, ⁻3, ⁻3, ⁻3, ⁻4, ⁻4, ⁻5, ⁻5;
   (d) ⁻5, ⁻4, ⁻4, ⁻3, ⁻3, ⁻3, ⁻2, ⁻2, ⁻1, 0, 0, 0, 0, 0, 0.

10 The diagrams in Figure 14 show the general shape of some frequency distributions.

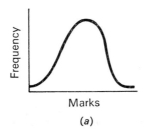 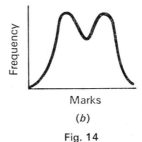 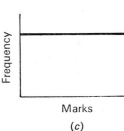

Marks   Marks   Marks
(a)   (b)   (c)

Fig. 14

What can you say about the modes in each case?

11 The contents of fifty boxes of matches of the same make were found to be as follows:

Number of matches	42	43	44	45	46	47	48
Number of boxes	10	6	20	6	5	2	1

What should the manufacturer state as the average number of matches per box?

12 Would measurements of the following quantities be exact or approximate?

(a) The distance from London to Glasgow;
(b) the weight of an apple;
(c) the amount of milk in a jug;
(d) the money in a bank account;
(e) the number of members in a club;
(f) the population of the world at any one time.

13 Would measurement of the following quantities give rise to continuous or discrete data?

(a) The numbers of people buying the various priced tickets to watch a football match.
(b) The amount of water used in a school kitchen during a day.
(c) The weights of pupils in a school.

14 Comment on the graph in Figure 15 and draw a 'better' one.

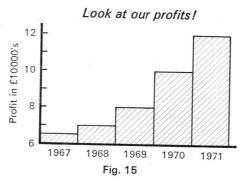

Look at our profits!

Fig. 15

15 A record was made of the yield of 100 potato plants with the following results:

Number of potatoes per plant	Number of plants (frequency)	Half-way value
1–5	10	
6–10	45	
11–15	36	
16–20	7	
21–25	2	

Copy and complete the last column of the table and so find the mean number of potatoes per plant.

16 The marks obtained by candidates in an examination were:

25, 83, 72, 60, 33, 34, 30, 21, 25, 74, 60, 42, 35, 32, 22,
27, 65, 84, 73, 14, 59, 65, 40, 19, 25, 2, 98, 83, 74, 37,
56, 21, 72, 47, 72, 46, 45, 20, 95, 4, 17, 62, 73, 84, 5,
27, 44, 42, 72, 65, 64, 85, 20, 29, 60, 52, 54, 55, 91, 92,
50, 65, 64, 61, 40, 37, 39, 48, 83, 75, 77, 65, 67, 55, 49,
78, 46, 63, 66, 52, 55, 64, 73, 54, 40.

(a) Find the exact mean directly from these marks.

(b) Draw up a grouped frequency table using the groups 0–9, 10–19, 20–29, etc. List the half-way value of each group and hence estimate the mean mark. Compare this with your answer to (a).

17 A survey was carried out on the life of car tyres under test conditions with the following results:

Number of km run before being worn out	Number of tyres
15000–17500	2
17501–20000	4
20001–22500	40
22501–25000	130
25001–27500	190
27501–30000	110
30001–32500	20
32501–35000	4

Draw a cumulative frequency graph and use it to estimate the median and quartiles.

18 The following grouped frequency table gives the percentage marks awarded in an examination:

Marks	Frequency
1–5	4
6–10	4
11–15	7
16–20	8
21–25	11
26–30	12
31–35	9
36–40	5
41–45	11
46–50	12
51–55	11
56–60	13
61–65	8
66–70	8
71–75	5
76–80	2

(a) Draw a bar chart to show how the marks were distributed and comment on its shape.

(b) Draw a cumulative frequency curve.

(c) Use your graph to find the median mark and the inter-quartile range.

(d) Use your graph to estimate the pass mark if only 40% of the candidates passed the examination.

19 Two small firms each have a total pay-roll of 100 people. The annual wages paid by these firms are given in the following table.

Annual wage in £		800	1000	1200	1500	1800	2000	3000	5000	10000
Number of people paid this wage	Firm A	15	25	35	16	3	3	1	1	1
	Firm B	35	25	20	10	0	3	2	4	1

(a) State the modal wage paid by each firm.

(b) State the median wage paid by each firm.

(c) Calculate the mean wage paid by each firm.

(d) A wage dispute arises and a plan for its settlement involves the comparison of the wages paid by the two firms. Which of the three 'averages' which you have calculated above would *you* use to compare the wages? Give your reasons for choosing this one and rejecting the others.

PROBABILITY

1 State the probability of throwing a number greater than 4 with one throw of an ordinary die.

2 A card is selected at random from a pack of 52 cards. State the probability:
(a) that the card is a queen;
(b) that the card is a heart;
(c) that the card is either a heart or a queen (or both).

3 You have four marbles in your pocket; three red and one blue. You take out three marbles. What is the probability that the marble left in your pocket is red?

4 A box contains 32 chocolates, some with hard centres and some with soft. If a chocolate is taken at random from the box, the probability that it has a hard centre is $\frac{1}{4}$. How many of the chocolates have soft centres?

5 A bag contains beads, some red, some white and some blue. If a bead is drawn at random from the bag, the probability that it is red is $\frac{1}{3}$ and the probability that it is white is $\frac{1}{4}$. What is the probability that it is blue?

6 I have four pieces of paper marked 3, 4, 5 and 9, respectively.
(a) How many different pairs of numbers can I select from these four numbers? List these pairs.

(*b*) I choose two of the four pieces at random. What is the probability that the numbers on these pieces will add to more than eight?

7   Figure 16 shows the numbers of netball, table-tennis and badminton players in a club. $N = $ {members who play netball}, $T = $ {members who play table-tennis} and $B = $ {members who play badminton}. Each member plays at least one of the three games.

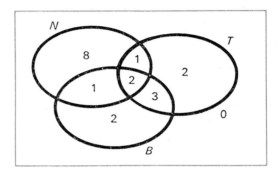

Fig. 16

(*a*) One of the members of the club is chosen at random. Find the probability that this member can play:
   (i)   badminton;
   (ii) table-tennis but not badminton;
   (iii) either table-tennis or netball (or both);
   (iv) both netball and badminton but not table-tennis.

(*b*) If a netball player is chosen at random, what is the probability that the player can also play table-tennis?

8   A jar contains 120 sweets: 30 are pink, 40 are yellow and 50 are white. A girl takes a sweet without looking.
   (*a*) What is the probability that it is pink?
   (*b*) What is the probability that it is not yellow?
   (*c*) If the girl actually takes a white sweet and eats it, what is the probability that her next sweet will also be white?

9   Two dice are made in the shape of regular tetrahedra, one with faces numbered 1 to 4, the other with faces numbered 5 to 8 (see Figure 17). They are thrown at the same time and the score is calculated by adding the numbers on the faces on which they land.

Fig. 17

Copy and complete the following table to give all the possible scores.

		Number on second die			
		5	6	7	8
Number on first die	1	6			
	2			9	
	3				
	4				

(a) Which is the most likely score?
(b) What is the probability of obtaining the highest possible score?
(c) What is the probability of scoring 7?
(d) What is the probability of scoring more than 9?
(e) What is the probability that the score is a prime number?

10 Two ordinary dice are thrown at the same time. Which of the following statements are true and which are false? If a statement is false, correct it.

(a) Throwing two sixes is less probable than throwing two fours.
(b) The probability that both dice show the same score is $\frac{1}{6}$.
(c) The most likely total score is 6.
(d) Throwing an even score and throwing an odd score are equally likely events.

(*Hint:* you may find it helpful to make a table which shows all the possible scores.)

11 A drawer contains four blue shirts and two white ones. Peter takes a shirt from the drawer and puts it on; then George takes one too. Both boys make their selection without looking at the colour.
    Copy and complete the tree diagram in Figure 18 and use it to find the probability that Peter and George:
(a) each select a blue shirt;   (b) select shirts of the same colour;
(c) select shirts of different colours.

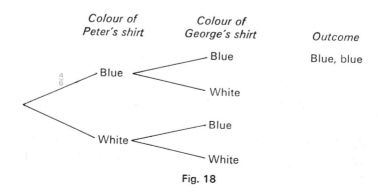

Fig. 18

12 Three unbiased coins are tossed. Find the probability that there will be 1 head and 2 tails.

13 A bag contains 20 discs: 12 yellow and 8 green. Two discs are taken out in succession and not replaced. By drawing a tree diagram, find the probability of taking two discs of different colours.

14 (a) Two unbiased coins are tossed. By drawing a tree diagram, find the probability that they will both be the same (that is, both heads or both tails).

(b) One unbiased coin is tossed together with a 'loaded' coin which has a probability of $\frac{2}{5}$ of landing heads and $\frac{3}{5}$ of landing tails. Find the probability that they will both be the same.

(c) Two biased coins are tossed, one with a probability of $\frac{2}{5}$, the other with a probability of $\frac{1}{3}$ of landing heads. What is the probability that they will both be the same?

15 A bag contains 5 red discs, 4 blue discs and 3 green discs. Single discs are drawn at random out of the bag in succession and not replaced. Find the probability that 2 blues and a red, in that order, are drawn from the bag in 3 draws.

16 A fairground stallholder earns his living by running a competition in which the public are invited to pay 10p for three table tennis balls.

A competitor rolls each ball in turn down a chute and they then drop at random into one of three slots. The slots are numbered one, two and three, and a ball earns a number of points according to the slot it enters. Therefore the highest total a competitor can obtain is 9, $(3+3+3)$ and the lowest total is 3, $(1+1+1)$.

Certain total scores are rewarded with a prize worth 20p.

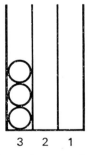
A total score of 9

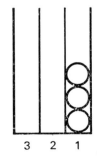
A total score of 3

(a) What is the probability that the first ball will enter the '3' slot?

(b) $3+3+1$ is one way of scoring seven with the three balls; $3+1+3$ is another. Altogether there are six ways of scoring a total of 7.

By any method, complete a copy of the following table:

Total score	9	8	7	6	5	4	3
Number of ways of scoring	1		6				1

(*c*) What is the probability of obtaining a total score of 6?

(*d*) What is the probability of obtaining a total score which is an even number?

(*e*) If you were the stallholder, for what total scores would you award prizes? Remember that you want to attract customers and also that you hope to make a living. *Justify your answer.*

CALCULATION

1 Use your slide rule to find the value of:

(*a*) $\dfrac{37 \cdot 5}{48 \cdot 3}$;

(*b*) $\sqrt{235}$;

(*c*) $2 \cdot 6 \times 3 \cdot 8 \times 4 \cdot 35$.

2 Express 0·00789 in standard form.

3 Find the value of: (*a*) $2^4 \times 3^2$;   (*b*) $\dfrac{7^4 \times 7^5}{7^7}$.

4 In a hotel the cost per person per day is £3·70. Calculate how much four people have to pay for 9 days. Give your answer to the nearest pound.

5 Express in standard form to 3 significant figures:

(*a*) 472690000;   (*b*) 0·0005457.

6 Use your slide rule to find to 2 significant figures:

(*a*) the value of $1 \cdot 76 \times 43 \cdot 2$;

(*b*) the number of German marks (D.M.) which can be bought for £80 if 1 D.M. is worth $10\frac{1}{2}$p.

7 Express the ratio 64 cm to 5 m in the form 1 to *x*, giving *x* to 2 significant figures.

8 Multiply $(3 \cdot 4 \times 10^6)$ by $(4 \cdot 5 \times 10^{-3})$ and give your answer in standard form.

9 If £1 is equivalent to 12 Swiss francs, what is the value of 50 Swiss francs? Give your answer to the nearest penny.

10 An aeroplane flies non-stop for $2\frac{3}{4}$ hours and travels 2400 km. Find its average speed in metres per second.

11 If the average length of my stride is 90 cm, find, to 2 significant figures, the number of strides I take in walking 2 km.

12

		Second number			
	$\times$	3·55	3·42	3·30	3·18
First number	3·55	12·6	12·1	11·7	11·3
	3·42	12·1	11·7	11·3	
	3·30	11·7	11·3	10·9	10·5
	3·18	11·3		10·5	10·1

The table shows the results, to 3 significant figures, when numbers in the first column are multiplied by the numbers in the first row.

(a) Multiply 3·42 by 3·18 as accurately as your slide rule permits and use your answer to complete a copy of the above table.

(b) From the table, find the value of $(3·42)^2$.

(c) Use the above table to find the value of $10·5 \div 3·30$.

(d) Use the table to calculate 355×318 and give your answer in standard form.

13 Box R says 'Give n the value 2'. Box S says 'Give x three times the value of n'. Thus Box S gives x the value 6.

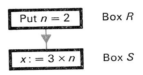

Put $n = 2$ Box R

$x := 3 \times n$ Box S

(a) Follow the instructions in the flow diagram below and write down the six numbers you obtain.

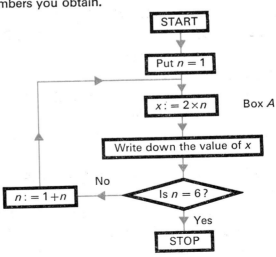

START

Put $n = 1$

$x := 2 \times n$ Box A

Write down the value of x

$n := 1 + n$ No   Is $n = 6$?

Yes

STOP

(b) What numbers would you have obtained if the instruction in Box A had been $x := 2 + n$?

(c) Make a change in Box A to obtain the numbers 1, 4, 9, 16, 25, 36.

Matrices

MATRICES

1 $P = \begin{pmatrix} 1 & 0 \\ 0 & -3 \\ 3 & 1 \end{pmatrix}$ and $Q = \begin{pmatrix} 1 & -1 & 2 \\ 2 & -3 & 4 \end{pmatrix}$.

(a) Find PQ.
(b) Find QP.
(c) What do your answers to (a) and (b) tell you about matrix multiplication?

2 What translation would map (2, 7) onto (5, 3)? Onto what point would the translation map (-2, 1)?

3 Find values of a, b, c, d so that

$$\begin{pmatrix} a & -1 \\ 6 & 2 \end{pmatrix} + \begin{pmatrix} 2 & b \\ c & -7 \end{pmatrix} = \begin{pmatrix} 5 & -5 \\ 3 & d \end{pmatrix}.$$

4 Work out:

(a) $(3 \quad 4 \quad 0) \begin{pmatrix} 1 & -1 & 0 \\ 0 & 0 & -1 \\ 2 & 0 & 1 \end{pmatrix} \begin{pmatrix} 4 \\ 0 \\ 3 \end{pmatrix}$;

(b) $(2 \quad -1 \quad -3) \begin{pmatrix} 4 & -1 & 1 \\ 1 & 0 & 1 \\ -1 & 3 & 0 \end{pmatrix} \begin{pmatrix} -1 \\ 1 \\ 2 \end{pmatrix}$.

5 This one-stage route matrix represents a network of roads:

$$\begin{array}{c} & & \text{To} \\ & & A \quad B \quad C \quad D \\ \text{From} & \begin{matrix} A \\ B \\ C \\ D \end{matrix} & \begin{pmatrix} 0 & 2 & 1 & 1 \\ 1 & 0 & 1 & 0 \\ 0 & 1 & 0 & 0 \\ 2 & 1 & 1 & 0 \end{pmatrix}. \end{array}$$

(a) Draw the network.
(b) Is it possible to reach D from C? If so, describe the route. If not, give a reason.

6 **A** is a 2 by 3 matrix.

(a) If $A + B = C$, what can you say about the order of (i) **B**; (ii) **C**?
(b) If $AD = E$, what can you say about the order of (i) **D**; (ii) **E**?

7 $P = \begin{pmatrix} 3 & 0 \\ 0 & 1 \end{pmatrix}$ and $Q = \begin{pmatrix} \frac{1}{3} & 0 \\ 0 & 1 \end{pmatrix}$.

(a) Work out PQ.
(b) What does your answer to (a) tell you about the transformations represented by the matrices **P** and **Q**?

8   Three lorries A, B and C carry crates of beer, cider, lemonade and orangeade.

Lorry A carries 60 crates of beer.

Lorry B carries 20 crates of beer, 25 crates of cider and 20 crates of lemonade.

Lorry C carries 30 crates of cider, 10 crates of lemonade and 25 crates of orangeade.

(a) Write this information as a 3 by 4 matrix.

(b) Each crate of beer weighs 12 kg, each crate of cider weighs 10 kg and each crate of lemonade or orangeade weighs 9 kg.

Express these weights as a 4 by 1 matrix.

(c) Use your matrices to find the weight in kilogrammes carried by each of the lorries.

9   $A = \begin{pmatrix} 1 & 0 \\ 0 & 2 \end{pmatrix}$, $B = \begin{pmatrix} -1 & 1 \\ 0 & -2 \end{pmatrix}$ and $C = \begin{pmatrix} 2 & -3 \\ -1 & 0 \end{pmatrix}$.

(a) Work out $A(BC)$.

(b) Work out $(AB)C$.

(c) Which property of the multiplication of matrices is illustrated by the answers to (a) and (b)?

10   Figure 19 shows the relation 'is the sister of' on the set of four children $\{a, b, c, d\}$.

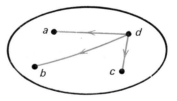

Fig. 19

(a) Which of the children are boys?

(b) Draw a diagram to show the relation 'has as brother' on the same set.

(c) Write down the matrix which represents the relation 'has as brother'.

11   The translation $\begin{pmatrix} -2 \\ -1 \end{pmatrix}$ is followed by the translation $\begin{pmatrix} -3 \\ 3 \end{pmatrix}$. What 2 by 1 matrix represents the combined translation?

12   $A = \begin{pmatrix} 1 & 0 \\ 2 & -1 \\ -3 & 2 \end{pmatrix}$. Write down the transpose of A. Call it A'.

Work out (i) AA'; (ii) $A'A$.

13   Find values of p and q so that $\begin{pmatrix} p & 5 \\ 4 & q \end{pmatrix}\begin{pmatrix} 2 \\ 1 \end{pmatrix} = \begin{pmatrix} 7 \\ 3 \end{pmatrix}$.

14 The matrix $\begin{pmatrix} 1 & \frac{3}{2} \\ 0 & 1 \end{pmatrix}$ describes the transformation which maps *OABC* onto *OA'B'C'* (see Figure 20).

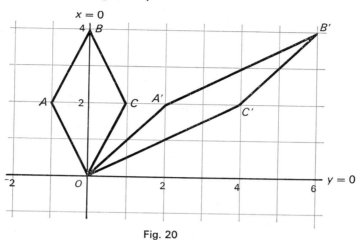

Fig. 20

(*a*) What type of transformation does the matrix represent?
(*b*) By describing the inverse transformation, find the matrix which maps *OA'B'C'* onto *OABC*.
(*c*) Find the areas of *OABC* and *OA'B'C'*.

15 Write down the one-stage route matrix for the network in Figure 21.

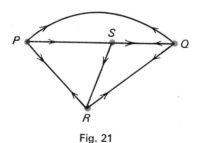

Fig. 21

Work out the two-stage and three-stage route matrices for this network. How many three-stage routes are there from *P* to *R*? List these routes.

16 The matrices $\mathbf{H} = \begin{pmatrix} 1 & 2 \\ 0 & 1 \end{pmatrix}$, $\mathbf{J} = \begin{pmatrix} 0 & -1 \\ 1 & 0 \end{pmatrix}$ and $\mathbf{K} = \begin{pmatrix} 2 & 0 \\ 0 & -1 \end{pmatrix}$ represent transformations.
    Draw diagrams to show the effect on the unit square of each of the following transformations:
(*a*) **HJ**; (*b*) **JH**; (*c*) **HK**.

17 $A = \begin{pmatrix} 1 & 0 \\ 0 & 1 \end{pmatrix}$, $B = \begin{pmatrix} 1 & 0 \\ 0 & -1 \end{pmatrix}$, $C = \begin{pmatrix} -1 & 0 \\ 0 & 1 \end{pmatrix}$ and $D = \begin{pmatrix} -1 & 0 \\ 0 & -1 \end{pmatrix}$.

(*a*) Describe geometrically the transformations represented by each of the matrices **A**, **B**, **C** and **D**.

(*b*) Copy and complete the following operation table for the set {**A, B, C, D**} under matrix multiplication.

Matrix multiplication	Second matrix			
First matrix	A	B	C	D
A				
B			D	
C				
D		C		A

(*c*) Use your table to answer the following questions.

(i) Is {**A, B, C, D**} closed under matrix multiplication? Give a reason for your answer.

(ii) Which element is the identity?

(iii) What are the inverses, if any, of **A, B, C, D**?

(iv) Give an example to show that matrix multiplication is associative for the set {**A, B, C, D**}.

(v) Is matrix multiplication commutative for the set {**A, B, C, D**}? Give a reason for your answer.

18 Investigate the geometrical effect of the matrix $\begin{pmatrix} a & 0 \\ 0 & 1 \end{pmatrix}$ where *a* is an integer, that is, *a* is a whole number.

MISCELLANEOUS

Computation 1

1 $3 \cdot 8 \times 342$.

2 $(97 \times 22) \div 0 \cdot 2$.

3 $3\frac{3}{4} + 2\frac{1}{3} - 1\frac{5}{6}$.

4 The value of $2 \cdot 5 \times \cos 69 \cdot 8°$.

5 $(15)^2 + (1 \cdot 5)^2 + (0 \cdot 15)^2$.

6 $\begin{pmatrix} 1 & 3 \\ 2 & 0 \end{pmatrix} \begin{pmatrix} 4 \\ 1 \end{pmatrix}$.

Computation 2

1 $-3(-5 - -4)$.

2 $14555 \div 410$.

3 $1\frac{2}{5} \div \frac{4}{5}$.

4 $\frac{22}{7} \times (0 \cdot 84)^2$.

5 $\frac{8}{9}$ of £7380.

6 $\dfrac{4 \cdot 5 \times 3 \cdot 66}{0 \cdot 06 \times 15}$.

Slide Rule Session No. 1

1 $5 \cdot 3 \times 1 \cdot 4$.

2 $9 \cdot 5 \div 1 \cdot 7$.

3 $(2 \cdot 7)^2$.

4 $7700 \div 0 \cdot 53$.

5 $\sqrt{130}$.

6 $\pi \times (3 \cdot 5)^2$.

7 $14 \times \sqrt{1700}$.

8 $0 \cdot 465 \div 0 \cdot 001\,72$.

9 $148 \times 33 \times 2 \cdot 5$.

10 $\dfrac{6 \cdot 5}{46 \times 0 \cdot 72}$.

Slide Rule Session No. 2

1 47×15.

2 $128 \div 2 \cdot 4$.

3 $0 \cdot 675 \times 3 \cdot 6$.

4 $(0 \cdot 82)^2$.

5 $\sqrt{0 \cdot 044}$.

6 $24 \cdot 4 \div 0 \cdot 673$.

7 16^3.

8 $\sqrt{(72 \times 16)}$.

9 $9 \cdot 8 \times 11 \cdot 7 \times 13 \cdot 6$.

10 $\dfrac{48 \cdot 5 \times 0 \cdot 4}{36}$.

In Exercises A and B there may be more than one correct answer to a question. Write down the letter or letters corresponding to the correct answer (or answers). Show any working that you do.

Exercise A (Multi-choice)

1 75% as a fraction is:
   (a) $\frac{3}{4}$;   (b) $\frac{4}{3}$;   (c) $\frac{25}{100}$;   (d) none of these.

2 If 63% of a class pass an examination, then the percentage which fail is:
   (a) 6·3;   (b) 63;   (c) 3·7;   (d) 37.

3 1101_{two} in base ten is:
   (a) 13;   (b) 3;   (c) 26;   (d) none of these.

4 In the figure, $\cos a°$ is:
   (a) $\frac{3}{4}$;
   (b) $\frac{3}{5}$;
   (c) $\frac{5}{4}$;
   (d) $\frac{4}{5}$.

5 Which of these fractions is closest in value to 2·15?
   (a) $2\frac{2}{5}$;   (b) $2\frac{1}{7}$;   (c) $2\frac{2}{9}$;   (d) $2\frac{3}{10}$.

6 If $2^x = 8$ then x is:
   (a) 4;   (b) 2;   (c) 3;   (d) $\frac{1}{4}$.

7 State which has the largest area:
   (a) a circle of radius 2 cm;
   (b) a square of side $3\frac{1}{2}$ cm;
   (c) a triangle whose sides are 3 cm, 4 cm, 5 cm;
   (d) a semi-circle of radius 4 cm.

8 Figure 22 shows the speed-time graph of a particle moving for 20 seconds. Which of the following statements are true?

(a) The initial speed is 10 cm/s.
(b) The total distance covered is 225 cm.
(c) During the last 10 seconds the particle is slowing down at a rate of 10 cm/s.
(d) The maximum speed reached is 20 cm/s.

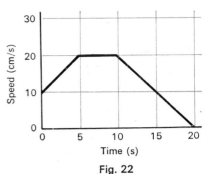

Fig. 22

Exercise B (Multi-choice)

1 $\frac{24}{30}$ is equivalent to:

(a) $\frac{6}{10}$;   (b) $\frac{4}{5}$;   (c) $\frac{2}{3}$;   (d) $\frac{12}{15}$.

2 23_{four} in base six is:

(a) 35;   (b) 15;   (c) 11;   (d) 53.

3 $\frac{1}{2} + \frac{2}{5} + \frac{2}{3}$ is:

(a) $\frac{5}{10}$;   (b) $\frac{4}{10}$;   (c) $\frac{47}{30}$;   (d) $\frac{31}{30}$.

4 The height of a boy is 1 m and that of his father is 200 cm. The ratio of the height of the boy to that of his father is:

(a) 1 to 200;   (b) 200 to 1;   (c) 1 to 20;   (d) 1 to 2.

5 A stopwatch is known to lose by exactly 1%. This means that:

(a) after 99 s it reads 100 s;   (b) after 100 s it reads 99 s;
(c) after 100 s it reads 101 s;   (d) after 101 s it reads 100 s.

6 The shaded area in Figure 23 represents:

(a) $(C \cup A) \cap B$;
(b) $C \cap (A \cup B)$;
(c) $C \cup (A \cap B)$;
(d) $(C \cup B) \cap A$.

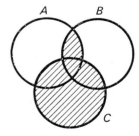

Fig. 23

7 If $A(2, 3)$, $B(^-1, 2)$, $C(^-2, ^-1)$ are three vertices of a parallelogram $ABCD$, then D is:

(a) (1, 0);   (b) ($^-1$, 4);   (c) (0, 1);   (d) none of these.

8 The transformation represented by the matrix $\begin{pmatrix} 0 & 1 \\ -1 & 0 \end{pmatrix}$ is:

   (*a*) a clockwise quarter-turn about the origin;
   (*b*) a half-turn about the origin;
   (*c*) reflection in the line $y = 0$;
   (*d*) reflection in the line $x = 0$.

Exercise C

1 What is the order of rotational symmetry of:

   (*a*) an equilateral triangle;   (*b*) a regular hexagon;
   (*c*) a parallelogram?

2 Add together 3·87, 0·2485, 0·083, 370. Now write your answer:

   (*a*) correct to 2 significant figures;
   (*b*) correct to 2 decimal places.

3 30% of a number is 36. Express 30% as a fraction and hence find the number.

4 Convert the following numbers into base ten:

   (*a*) 145_{six};   (*b*) 1101_{two};   (*c*) 181_{nine}.

5 Seven boys obtained the following marks out of 20 in a test: 12, 10, 17, 9, 15, 16, 6. The pass mark was 11. Find the probability that a boy chosen at random passed the test.

6 If we add the numbers in each row of Pascal's triangle we get:

$$1 = 1$$
$$1+1 = 2$$
$$1+2+1 = 4$$
$$1+3+3+1 = 8 \quad \text{and so on.}$$

   (*a*) What are the numbers in the fifth row?
   (*b*) What is the sum of the numbers in the tenth row?

7 Onto what point is ($^-$3, 5) mapped by the translation $\begin{pmatrix} -1 \\ -2 \end{pmatrix}$?

8 A supply of sugar was expected to last a camp of 20 people for 6 days of a holiday, but 5 of these people decided not to come. For how long would the sugar now be expected to last?

Exercise D

1 What is the equation of the line on which the points (1, 4), (3, 6) and (6, 9) lie?

2 State whether each of the following is true or false:

   (*a*) $\sqrt{6\cdot4} = 8$;   (*b*) $\sqrt{0\cdot64} = 0\cdot8$;
   (*c*) $\sqrt{0\cdot004} = 0\cdot02$;   (*d*) $\sqrt{0\cdot0036} = 0\cdot06$;
   (*e*) $\sqrt{0\cdot0144} = 0\cdot12$;   (*f*) $\sqrt{0\cdot016} = 0\cdot04$.

159

3   What are the coordinates of A in Figure 24?

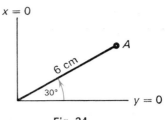

Fig. 24

4   If $v = u + at$, find:

(a) v if $u = 100$, $a = {}^-32$ and $t = 3$;

(b) t if $v = 200$, $u = 40$ and $a = 32$.

5   A storage tank is 40% full of petrol. If it contains 700 litres at present, how many litres will it hold altogether?

6   Put these numbers in order of size with the smallest first:

$$31_{five}, \quad 16_{seven}, \quad 120_{three}, \quad 22_{six}.$$

7   The two shortest sides of a right-angled triangle are 5 cm and 8 cm. Calculate the size of the smallest angle.

8   Solve each of the following equations:

(a) $2x + 7 = 9$;   (b) $3x - 1 = {}^-8$;   (c) $\frac{1}{2}x - 3 = 2$;

(d) $4(x + 3) = 16$;   (e) $8 - x = 12$;   (f) $\dfrac{10}{x} = 20$.

Exercise E

1   A straight line passes through the points (3, 2) and (7, 7). What is the gradient of the line?

2   Write down the value of:

(a) $0 \cdot 4 \times 0 \cdot 4$;   (b) $0 \cdot 03 \times 0 \cdot 05$;   (c) $0 \cdot 08 \div 0 \cdot 002$.

3   A cube has a volume of 125 cm³. What is its total surface area?

4   The flow diagram shows how to convert degrees Celsius to degrees Fahrenheit.

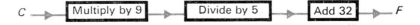

Draw the inverse flow diagram and use it to convert 79° Fahrenheit to degrees Celsius.

5   A 12 m ladder reaches 8 m up a wall. What is the angle the ladder makes with the ground?

6 $E = \{$quadrilaterals$\}$ and $F = \{$triangles, squares, rectangles, pentagons$\}$. What are the members of $E \cap F$?

7 Onto what point is (2, 1) mapped by:
   (*a*) a rotation of 180° about (0, 0);
   (*b*) reflection in the line $x = 0$?

8 A bag contains 30 coloured balls, all of the same size and material. If 9 balls are green, 13 are yellow and the rest are red, what is the probability of drawing a red ball out of the bag?

Exercise F

1 Write down the value of each of the following:
   (*a*) £3·74 to the nearest pound;
   (*b*) 525 cm to the nearest metre;
   (*c*) $3\frac{5}{8}$ to the nearest whole number;
   (*d*) 10·73 correct to 2 S.F.;
   (*e*) 11·96 correct to 1 decimal place.

2 Find the coordinates of the point (3, 2) after reflection in the line $y = 0$ followed by an anticlockwise turn about the origin through 90°.

3 Write the following as decimals:
   (*a*) $\frac{1}{5}$;   (*b*) $\frac{3}{8}$;   (*c*) $\frac{5}{6}$;   (*d*) $\frac{13}{40}$;   (*e*) $\frac{3}{11}$.

4 £3 is divided between three children aged 5, 7 and 8 years in the ratio of their ages. How many pence will each child receive?

5 A model of a ship is made on a scale of 1 to 50.
   (*a*) If the ship is 250 m long, what is the length of the model?
   (*b*) If the deck area of the model is 12 m², what is the deck area of the ship?

6 Find values of x and y so that $\begin{pmatrix} 3 & 0 \\ 1 & 2 \end{pmatrix} \begin{pmatrix} x \\ y \end{pmatrix} = \begin{pmatrix} 6 \\ 8 \end{pmatrix}$.

7 Using graph paper, draw accurately a net for the solid in Figure 25.

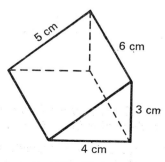

Fig. 25

161

8   A straight line passes through the points (1, 4) and (5, 12).

(*a*) Find its gradient.

(*b*) Find the coordinates of the point at which the line meets $x = 0$.

Exercise G

1   The heights of 11 men were measured in centimetres. They were recorded as:

180, 182, 180, 175, 170, 172, 174, 178, 185, 174, 180.

Find: (*a*) the median height;   (*b*) the modal height.

2   How many planes of symmetry has a regular tetrahedron?

3   Three out of a box of ten ball-point pens are defective. What is the probability that a customer buying two pens at random gets two good ones?

4   If the following addition sum is correct, which number base has been used?

$$\begin{array}{cccc} 2 & 3 & 4 & 5 \\ & 3 & 2 & 3 \\ 1 & 5 & 1 & 2 \\ \hline 4 & 5 & 1 & 3 \end{array}$$

5   Between which two consecutive whole numbers does $\sqrt{190}$ lie?

6   $A = \{\text{Factors of } 24\}$ and $B = \{\text{Factors of } 60\}$.

(*a*) List the members of A.   (*b*) List the members of B.

(*c*) List the members of $A \cap B$. Describe this set in words.

7   A set of glasses are all the same shape. The sherry glasses are of height 8 cm and their rims have diameter 4 cm. The wine glasses have rims of diameter 6 cm. How high are they? How many times greater is the capacity of a wine glass than that of a sherry glass?

8   $\mathbf{a} = \begin{pmatrix} 1 \\ 2 \end{pmatrix}$, $\mathbf{b} = \begin{pmatrix} -3 \\ 6 \end{pmatrix}$, and $\mathbf{c} = \begin{pmatrix} 2 \\ -7 \end{pmatrix}$.

Find:

(*a*) $5\mathbf{a}$;   (*b*) $\frac{1}{2}\mathbf{b}$;   (*c*) $\mathbf{b}+\mathbf{c}$;

(*d*) $\mathbf{a}+\mathbf{b}+\mathbf{c}$;   (*e*) $3(\mathbf{a}+\mathbf{b})$;   (*f*) $3\mathbf{a}+3\mathbf{b}$.

Exercise H

1   Taking the value of π from your slide rule, find the area of a sector of $57°$ cut from a circle of radius 4·64 cm.

2   What is the lowest set of five consecutive numbers you can find, none of these numbers being a prime number?

3 (a) Some networks are traversable. What does 'traversable' mean?

   (b) Sketch, if possible, networks with only:

     (i) one 4-node, one 3-node and one 1-node;

     (ii) one 5-node, two 3-nodes and one 1-node;

     (iii) one 5-node, one 4-node and one 1-node.

   (c) Which of the networks are traversable?

4 The bob of a pendulum which is 60 cm long rises 5 cm above the lowest point during a half-swing. What is the angle through which it swings?

5 If $a * b$ means 'multiply a by 3 and add b to the result', calculate:

   (a) $2 * 9$;   (b) $2 * (6 * 3)$;   (c) the value of x if $x * 7 = 22$.

6 Given that the area of square $ABCD$ is 8 km² write down:

   (a) the area of square $PQRS$;

   (b) the perimeter of square $PQRS$.

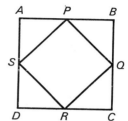

7 If $n(X) = 9$ and $n(Y) = 7$, what is the greatest possible value of $n(X \cup Y)$? What is the least possible value? Draw diagrams to illustrate each of these cases.

8 Solve each of the following equations:

   (a) $5x + 2 = 7$;   (b) $3x - 3 = {}^-5$;   (c) $7 - 2x = 13$;

   (d) $\dfrac{4}{x} + 1 = 9$;   (e) $2\left(\dfrac{3}{x} + 4\right) = 10$;   (f) $8 - \dfrac{5}{x} = {}^-2$.

Exercise I

1 (a) Sketch a square-based pyramid.

   (b) Draw accurately a net for a square-based pyramid for which the perimeter of the base is 12 cm and each of the remaining edges is 5 cm.

   (c) State the number of edges, vertices and faces of the pyramid you have sketched. What is the relation between them?

2 From the first 40 envelopes opened, the following donations were received as the result of an appeal:

Amount in £	25	20	15	10	5	2	1
Number of envelopes		1	4	1	9	15	5	5

   (a) Write down the most usual donation. What is the name of this kind of average?

   (b) Calculate the arithmetic mean of the distribution.

163

Revision exercises

3   A building has a flagpole on top as shown in Figure 26. The angle of elevation of the top of the building from a point 55 m from the foot of the building and on the same level is 42°. From the same point the angle of elevation of the top of the flagpole is 44·2°. Calculate:

(a) the height of the building to 2 s.f.;

(b) the length of the flagpole to the nearest metre.

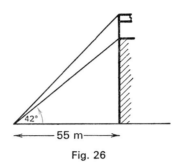

Fig. 26

4   Draw the graph of $y = x^2 + 3x + 4$ for values of x from ⁻5 to 2.

(a) What is the equation of the line of symmetry of this curve?

(b) Use your graph to solve the equations:

(i) $x^2 + 3x + 4 = 2$;   (ii) $x^2 + 3x + 4 = 8$;

(iii) $x^2 + 3x + 4 = 12$.

Exercise J

1   (a) Find the sum and the difference of 35_{seven} and 26_{seven}.

(b) Express 26_{ten} in (i) base 8; (ii) base 2.

(c) If 35 is equal to 38_{ten}, what number base is being used?

(d) Explain why 26 must represent an even number whatever base is being used?

2   (a) Using a scale of 1 cm to 1 unit, label axes from ⁻6 to 6. Draw the quadrilateral whose vertices are A (2, ⁻1), B (6, 0), C (4, 3) and D (2, 3).

(b) On your diagram show the image $A_1 B_1 C_1 D_1$ of the quadrilateral $ABCD$ under the transformation represented by $\mathbf{M} = \begin{pmatrix} 0 & -1 \\ 1 & 0 \end{pmatrix}$.

(c) Describe the transformation which $\mathbf{M}$ represents.

(d) Work out $\mathbf{M}^4$ and explain your result.

3   Figure 27 shows a model of a church. The slant edges of the roof are equal in length.

(a) Calculate the volume of the model.

(b) Calculate the total area of the slanting roof.

164

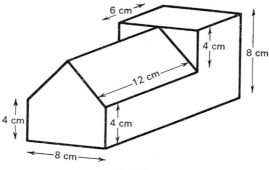

Fig. 27

4   In a C.S.E. examination all the pupils in a class of 30 were entered for
at least one of the subjects geography, history and French. 11 were
entered for history, 17 for geography and 15 for French. 5 were
entered for history and French but no candidate took both history and
geography.

Show this information on a diagram and find the number of
candidates who took both French and geography.

Exercise K

1   Solve each of the following equations:

(a) $\frac{1}{2}(5x+1) = 1$;   (b) $\frac{1}{3}x - \frac{1}{2} = 6$;   (c) $4(7-3x) = 16$;

(d) $7(8-x) = 14$;   (e) $-2 + \frac{3}{x} = 4$;   (f) $\frac{1}{2} - \frac{3}{x} = 3\frac{1}{2}$.

2   The following readings were taken from the instruments of an electric
train as it travelled between two stations:

Time in minutes	0	$\frac{1}{2}$	1	$1\frac{1}{2}$	2	$2\frac{1}{2}$	3	$3\frac{1}{2}$
Speed in metres per minute	0	900	1500	1780	1670	1360	750	0

(a) Draw a graph of speed against time. Use a scale of 4 cm to
1 minute on the axis across the page and 1 cm to 100 m/min on the
axis up the page.
(b) From your graph, estimate:
    (i) the speed after $1\frac{1}{4}$ minutes;
    (ii) when the speed was 1200 m/min.
(c) Estimate the area under the curve and state clearly what this
represents.

3   The chart in Figure 28 shows the frequency distribution of goals scored
this season by the Winton hockey team. Use the chart to find:

(a) the total number of matches played;
(b) the total number of goals scored;

(c) the mean number of goals per match;

(d) the probability that a spectator who watched only one match during the season saw Winton score (i) exactly four goals; (ii) at least four goals.

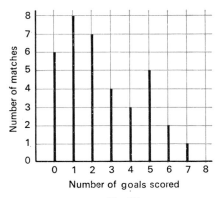

Fig. 28

4 On 1 January 1970 a man put £20 into a Savings Bank account. The interest rate was $3\frac{1}{2}$%.

(a) How much interest had he gained by the end of 1970?

(b) How much money was in his account by the end of 1970?

(c) In 1971 his interest was worked out on the amount of money in his account on 1 January 1971. How much money was in his account by the end of 1971? Give your answer to the nearest penny.

(d) Will the amount of money in his account at the end of 1972 be more or less than £22·10 or exactly £22·10? Give a reason for your answer.

Exercise L

1 (a) Copy and complete the 8 by 8 matrix **M** which represents the relation 'is a factor of' on the set of numbers {1, 2, 3, 4, 5, 6, 7, 8}.

$$
M = \begin{array}{c} \\ 1 \\ 2 \\ 3 \\ 4 \\ 5 \\ 6 \\ 7 \\ 8 \end{array}
\begin{array}{cccccccc}
1 & 2 & 3 & 4 & 5 & 6 & 7 & 8 \\
\left(\begin{array}{cccccccc}
1 & 1 & 1 & 1 & 1 & 1 & 1 & 1 \\
0 & 1 & 0 & 1 & 0 & & & \\
0 & 0 & 1 & 0 & 0 & & & \\
0 & 0 & 0 & 1 & 0 & & & \\
0 & 0 & 0 & 0 & 1 & & & \\
0 & 0 & 0 & 0 & 0 & & & \\
0 & 0 & 0 & 0 & 0 & & & \\
0 & 0 & 0 & 0 & 0 & & &
\end{array}\right)
\end{array}
$$

(b) What relation does the transpose of **M** represent?

(c) Work out (1 1 1 1 1 1 1 1) **M**.

(d) Explain the meaning of each of the entries in your answer to (c).

2 Figure 29 shows two spinners. The edges of the black spinner are numbered 1, 3, 4, 5, 7 and the edges of the red spinner are numbered 1, 2, 3, 4, 7.

Fig. 29

A game is played in which each spinner is spun once. The score is found by adding the numbers on the edges which fall in contact with the table on which the game is played.

(a) Copy and complete the following table of scores.

		Number on red spinner				
		1	2	3	4	7
Number on black spinner	1	2				
	3				7	
	4					
	5					
	7					

(b) Which is the most likely score?

(c) What is the probability of scoring 8?

(d) To win the game you must score 8. If you were given the choice of spinning once with each spinner or twice with either the black or the red spinner, what would you choose to do?

Explain your answer carefully.

3

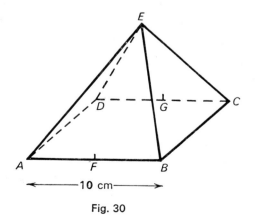

E is at a distance of 13 cm from each of the corners of the square base.

Fig. 30

Figure 30 shows a square-based pyramid. This is suspended from the ceiling of a mathematics room. Flossy the fly (wife of Fred) is at *E*, and, being a mathematical fly, decides to find the lengths of various paths round the pyramid, each time starting and finishing at *E*.

(*a*) She goes from *E* to *B* to *A* to *E* along the edges. How far has she walked?

(*b*) She goes from *E* to *A* to *C* to *E*. How far has she walked?

(*c*) She goes from *E* to *F* to *G* to *E* (*F* and *G* are the mid-points of *AB* and *CD*). How far has she walked?

(*d*) Which is the shortest of these three paths? Sketch the pyramid and show on it another path which is the same length as this shortest path.

4 A large metal bolt is shown in Figure 31 (*a*). It is made of a cylindrical shaft fitted with a hexagonal-shaped head. This head is 12 mm thick. The shaft has a length of 50 mm and a radius of 7 mm. Figure 31 (*b*) shows the cross-section of the head of the bolt.

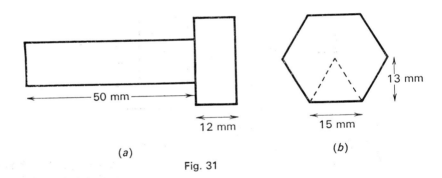

50 mm

12 mm

(*a*)

13 mm

15 mm

(*b*)

Fig. 31

(*a*) Find the volume of the shaft. (Take π to be $\frac{22}{7}$.)

(*b*) The hexagon can be split up into triangles of which one is marked. How many triangles will there be? What is the area of each triangle?

(*c*) What is the area of the hexagon?

(*d*) Find the volume of the hexagonal head and so work out the total volume of the bolt.

Exercise M

1 Figure 32 shows a cross-section of a mountain range. *A* and *B* are at sea level and 1 cm represents 1 km on both axes.

(*a*) What is the height above sea level of the highest point of the mountain range? Give your answer in *metres*.

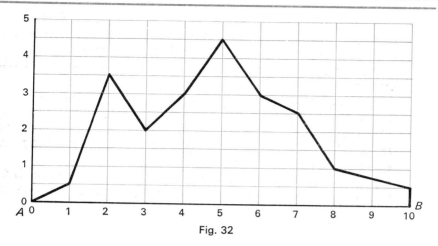

Fig. 32

(*b*) What is the gradient of the steepest slope in the mountain range, other than the vertical cliff at *B*?

(*c*) Calculate the area of the cross-section in square kilometres.

(*d*) What is the mean height of the cross-section?

2 Two aeroplanes leave an airport *A* at the same time, one travelling at 200 km per hour on a bearing of 050° from *A* and the other travelling at 300 km per hour on a bearing of 140° from *A*.

After $1\frac{1}{2}$ hours the first aeroplane lands at *B* and the second aeroplane lands at *C*. Draw a rough sketch to show their positions at this time. Calculate:

(*a*) the distance of *C* from *B*,   (*b*) the angle *ACB*.

3 Figure 33 shows a pyramid on a square base *ABCD* of side 12 cm. The vertex *V* is *vertically above A* and *VB* = 13 cm.

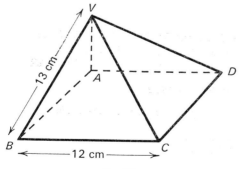

Fig. 33

(*a*) State the number of faces of the pyramid.

(*b*) State the number of faces which are right-angled triangles.

(*c*) Calculate the height (*VA*) of the pyramid.

(*d*) Calculate the total surface area of the pyramid.

169

4   A small firm builds sheds and greenhouses. A shed requires 2 hours of machine time and 5 hours of craftsman time. A greenhouse requires 3 hours of machine time and 5 hours of craftsman time.

The total machine time available is 12 hours per day and the total craftsmen time available is 25 hours per day.

Suppose the firm makes s sheds and g greenhouses per day.

(*a*) Write down two relations which must be true.

(*b*) Represent these relations on a graph, shading out the unwanted regions. Mark the points which represent the numbers of completed sheds and greenhouses that can be made in one day.

(*c*) If the profit on a shed is £5 and the profit on a greenhouse is £8, work out how the firm can make the largest possible profit in one day.

Published by the Syndics of the Cambridge University Press
Bentley House, 200 Euston Road, London NW1 2DB
American Branch: 32 East 57th Street, New York, N.Y.10022

Library of Congress Catalogue Card Number: 68–21399

ISBNs: 0 521 08419 9 limp covers
       0 521 08420 2 hard covers

Printed in Great Britain
at the University Printing House, Cambridge
(Brooke Crutchley, University Printer)